RECEIVED

D1012955

NO LONGER PROPERTY OF
SEATTLE PUBLIC LIBRARY

JUST SIT

JUST SiT

A MEDiTATiON GUiDEBOOK FOR PEOPLE WHO KNOW THEY SHOULD BUT DON'T

SUKEY NOVOGRATZ AND ELiZABETH NOVOGRATZ

iLLUSTRATiONS BY NiEGE BORGES

HARPER
WAVE

AN iMPRiNT OF HARPERCOLLiNSPUBLiSHERS

JUST SIT. Copyright © 2017 by Sukey Novogratz and Elizabeth Novogratz. All rights reserved. Printed in the United States of America. No part of this book may be used or reproduced in any manner whatsoever without written permission except in the case of brief quotations embodied in critical articles and reviews. For information, address HarperCollins Publishers, 195 Broadway, New York, NY 10007.

HarperCollins books may be purchased for educational, business, or sales promotional use. For information, please email the Special Markets Department at SPsales@harpercollins.com.

FIRST EDITION

Designed and illustrated by Niege Borges

Library of Congress Cataloging-in-Publication Data has been applied for.

ISBN 978-0-06-267286-5

17 18 19 20 21   LSC   10 9 8 7 6 5 4 3 2 1

TO OUR FAMILY

CONTENTS

WE'RE ALL
JUST WALKING
EACH OTHER
HOME

RAM DASS

One dusty sunlit evening in the summer of 1963, Elizabeth's father and Sukey's father-in-law, Robert Novogratz, went for his usual postwork run, hoping to shake off the day with a little sweat. Robert was a 26-year-old army officer, stationed outside of Detroit with his wife, Barbara, and their first two children. Not too many years earlier, Robert had been an All-American football player at West Point. Since then, and throughout his military training, he'd been committed to maintaining a disciplined exercise regimen.

On this particular evening he was a couple of miles away from home when a police car pulled up.

"Freeze!" one of the officers yelled. Then, to Robert's surprise, the two cops jumped out of the car and grabbed ahold of him.

"What are you running from?" one of them asked gruffly.

Robert, confused, stood frozen like he'd been told. "I'm exercising," he said.

The cops looked him over suspiciously. It was 1963. Regular people didn't just go out for a pre-dinner jog.

Robert took out his military identification and handed it over. "I swear, Officers, I'm just out for a run. I like it—it keeps me in shape and helps me to unwind after a hard day. That's all."

The officers continued to eye him warily.

"Okay, sir. We're not going to arrest you. But we are going to drive you home."

And so, like a common criminal, Robert got into the backseat of the police car. When they arrived at the house he'd said was his, the officers escorted him to the door to make sure. His wife verified his claim—and had a few questions for her husband after the officers left.

Today, this whole scenario seems laughable, especially now that most of us exercise, or at least acknowledge that it's a good thing to do. Meditation has now become the modern-day equivalent of what jogging was a few decades ago—though it's catching on in the mainstream, in many places it is still viewed with skepticism, even resistance or derision. As a culture, we're past the point of total denial of meditation's benefits, but not yet to the point of firm acceptance of it as a healthful practice in the same way as regular exercise or eating vegetables or not smoking. People might still look at you like you're crazy for sitting motionless on the floor, gazing off at nothing, but they probably won't call the cops.

Back in the 1960s, people didn't jog, and they ate artificially flavored gelatin and called it salad. Fifty years later, hundreds of thousands of Americans participate in marathons every year, and quinoa and leafy greens are considered staples of many of our diets. Fifty years from now, it very well may be that the practice of meditation is simply a given. Because anyone can do it, even you. So keep reading. Then put down this book and sit.

MEDITATION IS NOT FOR SISSIES

It's true what they say: Meditation will change your life. It can make you healthier, nicer, more patient, a better parent, a kinder and gentler spouse, more creative; it will lower your blood pressure and improve your sleep; it'll help you lose weight, lose wrinkles, have better sex, get through grief, deal with trauma, love more, and fight less. Meditation will make you shine.

On top of that, it doesn't require a huge time commitment; we're talking about only twenty minutes a day. That's less time than watching a sitcom or getting a manicure. And it doesn't cost anything. You don't need any special equipment. And the stigma that you are either a dirty hippie or a cult member (or both) if you meditate are long gone. So basically, meditation is awesome, and the rewards of the practice far outweigh the effort.

But there's one small catch: You actually have to do it. Planning to do it, talking about doing it, fantasizing about how blissed out you will be one day at the ashram . . . none of it counts. That's the bit that stops most people from meditating—the actual sitting and meditating.

So what gives? Why is it so hard to just show up?

We're assuming here that you aren't meditating, at least not on a daily basis—otherwise you wouldn't be reading a book about it. Here's the thing with meditation, once you learn how to do it and do it daily: suddenly all sorts of positive changes tend to come, and come faster and easier than ever (and they tend to be stickier, too). Meditation is the best tool for change that we know of. Whether you want to lose 20 pounds, leave a bad relationship, or just be nicer in traffic, meditation will help you get there. And the longer you do it, the less it feels like a chore, and the more it feels like a treat—so much so that most people actually start looking forward to showing up.

Often a crisis is what makes us realize that we need to change. Many people come to meditation because they're in the middle of a life overhaul or they've just experienced a cosmic smackdown, like divorce, infidelity, death, or some other kind of gut-wrenching trauma. Though painful, these events can be a perfect catalyst, because often they force us to get serious about change. If you are in the middle of a crisis, you also might want to consider seeing a therapist, psychologist, or social worker if you aren't already. But don't worry—personal tragedy is not required any more than a pair of designer superwicking organic bamboo fiber yoga pants is. The best thing about meditation is that you can come as you are, and today is a great day to get started.

Once upon a time the two of us (and a couple others) were running a website and sending a daily email that focused on all things wellness: yoga, kale, reflexology, DIY walnut body scrubs, essential oils, and so on. We had readers from all over the United States—folks who wanted a little humor along with solid information—and many of them wrote to us. Mostly they had questions (well, they had comments and suggestions, too). Some asked about recipes involving turmeric, some wanted to know about yoga for runners, and others hoped for some insight on sunscreen. But, far and away, most of our readers were thirsting for some information about meditation.

Most of these wary would-be sitters already knew that meditation would be good for their mental, physical, and emotional health; that there was an endless list of benefits; and that meditation would probably change their lives. But they didn't really get what meditation actually *was* and/or how to do it.

At the time, our own interest in meditation was growing. We had been on retreats and to workshops and classes; we'd read books on the subject; we'd spoken with gurus and monks and teachers. But as we combed through our readers' questions, we came face-to-face with how much we didn't know—because we didn't really meditate. At least, not every day and, to be honest, sometimes not every week, and sometimes only once or twice a month. In short, we talked a big game. Hell, we'd done at least 25 articles on it. At the same time we knew that until we actually slowed down and got disciplined and sat every single day, not only were we not practicing what we were preaching, we didn't truly have a good idea of what any of it really meant.

So we dug in. We wanted to know the answers to those questions as much as our readers did. If meditation was so great, then why wasn't everyone doing it? Can it really transform lives? What's all the medical hype about? Will it actually help with aging—like, the wrinkles and sagging kind of aging? What about parenting? And creativity? And patience? And self-acceptance?

To find the answers, there was just one thing left to do: sit. And research and travel and sit some more. We sat at home, at the office, on the road, in hotel rooms, at meditation retreats, in India, on the floor, on cushions, on sofas, in the grass, on the sand, on hikes. We sat and we learned and we talked to many people along the way. We saw that the biggest secret surrounding meditation is that there is no secret. You just show up every day and you sit.

At a certain point, we realized that there was more to be done than providing short, simple (and extremely cute, if you don't mind us saying) daily emails that took less than two minutes to digest. *JUST SIT* was born out of the questions we received from our friends, family, and digital community, augmented with in-depth background and research added to enrich the book and spice up the mix. We know that everyone on this planet would benefit from meditation—in fact, the world would be a much kinder place if we all slowed down and sat every day. This is why we put together this book: to take the mystery out of meditation, and to help you, our community, to get up the nerve to show up every day to sit, no matter what.

MEDITATION GOES WEST

Meditation has been around for 5,000 years, or possibly even longer, but just because something is ancient doesn't necessarily mean it's awesome. But we think that in this case it is.

400–100 BCE

An Indian named Patanjali wrote the *Yoga Sutras* and a how-to guide to go along with them. This practice is called Ashtanga—the Eight Limbs, including asana (poses), pranayama (breathing techniques), and a ton of meditation. It's been the go-to toolbox for yoga teachers everywhere since the beginning of time. Well, since 400 BCE.

1893

SWAMI VIVEKANANDA

arrived in Chicago and rocked the entire USA with his lectures on spirituality. The whole country fell in love with him. He introduced meditation to many Americans for the first time.

1967

THE BEATLES met

Maharishi Mahesh Yogi, the yogi who developed the Transcendental Meditation technique, and suddenly all of the cool kids everywhere were headed to the cushion. TM's popularity exploded in the West.

1971

RAM DASS wrote *Be Here Now*, the countercultural bible that woke many Americans from a deep slumber.

1975

THE RELAXATION RESPONSE

Herbert Benson was the first Western doctor to prescribe meditation. Hooray for Herbert!

1990

SEJI OGAWA DISCOVERED THAT THE FMRI

could be used to measure meditation's effects on the brain. The studies confirmed what yogis have been saying forever—meditation changes the brain's neuroplasticity. Duh.

1979

MINDFULNESS-BASED STRESS REDUCTION

was introduced to the West by Jon Kabat-Zinn.

1980

YODA meditated on the big screen. Soon after, aspiring Jedi Knights cropped up everywhere.

2014

Meditation becomes mainstream. February's issue of *Time* magazine is the Mindful Resolution.

CHAPTER 1

KEEP IT SIMPLE:
INSTRUCTIONS FOR SITTING

SO YOU'VE DECIDED THAT YOU WANT TO START MEDITATING

Maybe someone told you how great it is, that it would change your life. Maybe you've tried it in the past and it didn't go so well—after 60 seconds you started to feel like you were doing it wrong or the timing was off or your ankle bones hurt or that there was something more important you just had to attend to, like bleaching the bathtub. Or maybe it just felt too awkward or uncomfortable.

Guess what? That's normal. Every single person we know who has tried meditation confronts resistance to it.

Before most of us even get to step one—the actual sitting—we come up with all the reasons why we can't or won't do it: it's boring, we're too busy, we're too unholy or too inflexible or too hairy. Or we agree that it's great stuff . . . for other people.

The big nonsecret with meditation is that it can and usually does feel stupid, pointless, and counterproductive in the beginning. Starting something new and unknown can suck; it can make you feel vulnerable or uncomfortable; it can bring up all sorts of insecurities you'd just rather not deal with. Which is why, as adults, when we try something new, we so often quit before we give it a real chance.

The challenge isn't over once you do manage to take that first step. Showing up and being consistent can be even trickier. Instead of enduring the wobbly, exposed, why-on-earth-am-I-doing-this phase, we fall back into making excuses: we've given it a go, but it's too hard, it's a waste of time, it's not for me. Or we blame something outside of ourselves, like our schedule or our family—or we blame ourselves.

THE TRUTH IS: MEDITATION ISN'T THAT COMPLICATED

There's not a soul on the planet who couldn't benefit from meditation. It's probably the best gift you can give yourself, you just won't know that until you experience it. Then you'll ask yourself, Why did I wait so long? Not to worry—you can start right now and we'll help you.

YOU WEREN'T REALLY PROCRASTINATING

Perhaps you've already done a lot of thinking about meditation: you've read articles, downloaded guided sessions and apps, talked about it with friends, recommended it without actually knowing that much about it. During that time you haven't actually been meditating, but all of that effort has been more helpful than you think. It's a way of planting the seeds, of laying the groundwork. The problem is that this preparation and planning phase is a little too comfortable. It's very easy to move here and retire. That is where we come in: to wake you up and help you get from the couch to the cushion, out of the prepping phase and into the actual meditating phase. For real. Not for fake.

Meditation is a way of training your mind to slow down, to be responsive, not reactive, to bring you into your life and out of the constant chatter that's going on in your head. It is a workout for the mind, which means that it takes work, practice, and discipline in the same way that working out takes work, practice, and discipline. And, like working out, results do not come overnight. Results come after time and effort and consistency. You might feel better after your first day back in spin class, but a one-off probably won't help you to lose those ten postpartum pounds. It's the same with meditation.

Just like a new exercise program, you have to start, jump in, just do it. Enough with the procrastination, the talking about it, the thinking about it, the avoiding it. You already know how to meditate. It's in you.

So try it for 2 minutes. Set a timer right now and give it a shot. In the next section you will find simple instructions for sitting. After that, the next 7 chapters will help you to turn those 2 minutes into a lifetime of practice.

INSTRUCTIONS FOR SITTING

1
SIT

The specifics don't matter—sit in a chair, cross-legged on the floor, in a tree. Just sit.

2
CLOSE YOUR EYES

Or, if you prefer to keep them open, give them something to softly focus on, such as a candle or a spot on the wall.

3
ARMS AND HANDS

Relax and rest your hands on your thighs.

4
LEGS AND FEET

Keep a straight spine: If you are in a chair, keep your feet on the floor. If you're on a cushion, keep your knees below your hips.

5
SET A TIMER (YOUR PHONE IS GREAT)

Just don't forget to put it on airplane mode. Start with 2 minutes and increase the time from there.

6
WARM UP

Note what's going on in your body. How does your back feel? What about your legs? Take 10 deep breaths. This will activate your parasympathetic nervous system, like warming up preworkout.

7
TAKE A MOMENT

Pay attention to the thoughts that are racing around. Things like: *I don't have time for this right now. I should be saving the seals. This is stupid.* All of the chatter is normal and will probably intensify as you sit.

WHERE TO PLACE YOUR ATTENTION

BREATHE

Focus on your breath. Notice the sound of your breath as you inhale, the sound as you exhale, and notice the sensation of the rise and fall of your belly.

ANCHOR

An anchor can be words (a mantra), counting or tracking your breath, or an image (if your eyes are open). Sometimes it's easiest to use your breath and a mantra together as an anchor. There will be more details on this later, in chapter 6. For now, try this: While breathing in, mentally say, "Sat," while breathing out, mentally say, "Nam."

THOUGHTS will come and they'll come often. Notice if you get discouraged, frustrated, or annoyed—that's okay. The key word here is *gentleness*. Whenever you are able to recognize that you're thinking, gently bring your focus back to your breaths and let the thoughts slide away.

iNTRODUCiNG THE MOMENT OF NO

The second you sit down to meditate is usually the same second that resistance comes out of hiding to terrorize you. It is sneaky—so watch closely. With practice, what you'll start to realize is that resistance happens all day, every day, in many forms in our regular lives outside of meditation.

One of the many beauties of mediation is that, the more we do it, the easier it is to observe all the resistance going on in our messy little minds. And once we see it, its power starts to fade.

YOU'LL NOTICE THAT THE MiND CAN BE SiMiLAR TO AN UNRULY LiTTLE KiD WHO DOESN'T WANT TO EAT HiS DiNNER.

THE MOMENT OF NO

THE MOMENT OF NO (YES, THAT IS HIS NAME, KIND OF LIKE THE DUKE OF EARL) IS THE CREATURE THAT PERSONIFIES RESISTANCE. HE IS AN ENERGY VACUUM, AN ENABLER, AND A BULLY, BUT HE WILL APPEAR TO BE YOUR NUMBER-ONE FAN. HE THRIVES ON INSECURITY, ANXIETY, AND UNCERTAINTY.

HIS ENEMIES ARE HUMILITY, ACCEPTANCE, AND LETTING GO. HIS MOST POWERFUL OPPONENT IS MEDITATION. HE IS A SHAPE-SHIFTER, SO DON'T BE FOOLED. YOU NEED TO DEVELOP SUPERHERO-LIKE SKILLS TO RECOGNIZE AND OBSERVE HIM WHEN HE SHOWS UP. YOU MIGHT EVEN NEED X-RAY VISION. REMEMBER: HE'S A TRICKSTER AND IS THERE TO SHAKE YOU UP.

JUST-LOVE HIM!

THE MOMENT OF NO IS
RESISTANCE

BEWARE: THERE ARE A FEW SPOTS WHERE THE MOMENT OF NO LURKS

I DON'T HAVE TIME TO MEDITATE NOW, I'M TOO TIRED, I CAN'T SIT WITHOUT A CUSHION, I HAVE SO MUCH TO DO, I'M NOT IN THE MOOD, I DON'T WANT TO DEAL WITH THESE THOUGHTS

NO

I DON'T WANT TO TAKE AN ART CLASS, I SUCK AT PAINTING, I HATE THOSE PEOPLE, MY SCHEDULE IS CRAZY

HE'S NOT MY TYPE, HE'S TOO HOT/HIP/ TALL/SHORT FOR ME

NO, I CAN'T DANCE, I LOOK STUPID, MY BUTT JIGGLES WHEN I DO IT

NO, I AM NOT FEELING IT OR FEELING ON OR FEELING ALIVE

NO

NO, I DON'T HAVE THE TIME, MONEY, HELP, RESOURCES

NO, I SUCK AT SKATING, I CAN'T SWIM, I AM A SLOW RUNNER, I HAVE A BAD KNEE, I DON'T HAVE THE RIGHT CLOTHES WITH ME, I LEFT MY SHOES AT HOME, I AM LATE, I AM HUNGRY, I NEED A DRINK, I NEED A XANAX

NO

How do I deal with the Moment of No?

Sit and observe him. Watch him and maybe feed him lunch or a glass of wine and then send him on his way. This transforms the Moment of No into the Moment of Go—you can move through and beyond him; you are aware of him, but you don't have to take his orders.

YOUR JOB: OBSERVE. OBSERVE. OBSERVE.

DON'T FALL FOR IT

ANXIOUSNESS

Your mind loves to resist. Thoughts will likely run rampant in the beginning, and many of them will probably pertain to everything else you should or could be doing instead of meditating. This is resistance. This is normal.

RESTLESSNESS

Sensations in your body will come and go like thoughts in your mind. You might think, *Man, my knee hurts so bad that I have to get up and shake my leg.* Actually, your knee is fine; that's just resistance. Your mind is collaborating with your body to trick you. Breathe in the sensation, then breathe it out—it will change, perhaps even disappear. Think: *This, too, shall pass.* This is a fine metaphor for life, as all pain passes (well, most does). Watching your pain will build stamina for other areas of your life.

SLEEPINESS

You might get tired. Exhausted. Out of nowhere, like Dorothy-in-the-poppy-field tired. If this happens, check your posture. It sounds silly, but connecting with your body can help you to stay awake. Sit up straight; if sitting up straight is a problem, then sit on a pillow or sit leaning back against a wall. There's also a chance you might just need more sleep, which we recommend getting if you can, just not during meditation. You'll find that over time, meditation will actually increase your energy in a big way and will also help you get better sleep at night.

CONFUSED?

There are a lot of misconceptions about what meditation is and what it does. Many people come to it with unrealistic expectations and ideas. It might be easier to start with what it isn't and what not to expect.

WHAT MEDITATION ISN'T

A way to stop your thoughts or empty your mind.

Unless you're dead, the mind doesn't empty and thoughts don't stop. Meditation is a way to slow down and observe your mind, not kill it.

A cosmic light show.

That's what Burning Man is for.

A spiritual bliss-out.

Some people try meditation because they're looking for a spiritual orgasm. We haven't experienced that, but hey, who knows, you might. If you do, will you let us know? You know, for research's sake.

Absolute stillness.

Absolute anything doesn't really help. And anyway, what does "absolute stillness" even mean?

A 20-minute checkout from reality.

That's what TV is for.

A way to relax or tune out.

Pot, a strong drink, decorating your Pinterest board, falling into a K-hole: those are great ways to check out. Meditation is the opposite of taking drugs or surrendering to social media—it tunes you in.

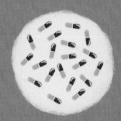

A happy pill.

Sorry, ain't no such thing. If there were, we'd all have taken it already.

WOE IS ME

I've tried to meditate multiple times over the past year. I sit on my living room floor, close my eyes, and feel like a fool. How do I get past it?

Well, of course you do. You are sitting on the floor, legs crossed, eyes closed, and . . . what? When is the last time you did any of that, kindergarten?

The ultimate question is: Who cares if you feel like a fool?

No one is watching you or posting your meditation session on Facebook. Step one to becoming a meditator: Get over yourself. Have fun with it.

HELPFUL TIPS TO ELIMINATE AWKWARDNESS

Look, starting out is going to feel awkward, period. Here are some ways to take the awkwardness out of it:

- Sit in a chair. You don't have to sit in the middle of the floor.
- Put on some music. Nothing too loud or crazy but something to keep you company.
- Use a blanket. This can make you feel cozy and safe, like a baby being swaddled.
- Download a guided meditation for something to focus on.
- Set a timer so that you have an end point.

PLEASE EXPLAIN

How does just sitting there help me to train my mind?

That depends on what you're sitting there doing. If you're meditating (or attempting to), you will probably notice the laundry list of boring obsessive thoughts that fight for your mind's attention. Just sitting and noticing these thoughts is the training. That is what meditation is. Yoda, Bruce Lee, and Gandhi all meditated before breakfast. That's the breakfast of champions. The thoughts are like pesky little pirates waiting to hook on to some narrative of yours, and then all of a sudden your poor brain has been hijacked. The funny thing is that watching those thoughts is what makes them go away. It takes you off autopilot and puts you back behind the steering wheel.

LAZY BRAIN

My mind is sharp already. So why would it need training?

We're not saying you're a dummy. We're saying that your mind might be out of shape, or conditioned to focus on unhelpful and prepackaged crap, or stuck in a rut. No offense. Meditation is a way to clean all that up, to shine a spotlight on those old habits and the useless junk that's been churning in your mind all day. Your mind might be sharp, but this is about building *wisdom*. Getting there involves a whole different muscle group.

IF YOU CAN BREATHE, YOU CAN SIT

Can anyone meditate?

A lot of people think meditation is great . . . for other people. They make up excuses. *It's not really me. I'm not that kind of person. I'm not a hippie. I'm not a monk.* Listen, all humans have the ability to breathe. For the past 5,000 years, millions of humans have done just that. No matter who you are, where you come from, who you sleep with, who you vote for, whether you live in a house, an apartment, or a yurt—you can, too. We all breathe. We can all meditate. It's that simple.

YOU CAN SIT FOR 20 MINUTES
(YOU DO IT ALL THE TIME)

DO i HAVE TO?

I keep hearing that meditation will change my life, but I'm just not a meditator. One of my friends is a painter, and she says that painting is her daily meditation. Could I do some activity like that instead and get similar results?

Sitting is sitting. There are a lot of activities that bring focus and stillness, but they aren't necessarily meditation. If you are painting and are completely absorbed by what you're doing, so much so that you're in a state of flow, well, hey, that's fantastic. Go ahead and paint away, create a masterpiece, get moved, be moved, move others—but you're not meditating, you're painting. Meditation is its own thing, a technique to study the mind without external stimuli.

Meditation is meditation.

i DON'T LiKE SURPRiSES

I am new to meditation. What can I or should I expect?

What you can expect is that you'll probably feel a little awkward, weird, uncomfortable, silly, unproductive; like you're bad at it, you're not doing it right, you're wasting time. At least, that's the case for many of us in the beginning. The trick is to do it again tomorrow and the next day, because it will change. And you will change. But it doesn't work if you don't show up.

BREATHALYZER

Should I breathe deeply? So that I can hear it?

Breathe normally and focus on the breath. Follow it in, follow it out. There are many breathing practices and exercises that are helpful in certain situations, but for everyday meditation, just breathe.

TIPS FOR NEWBIES (AND OLDIES)

- KEEP IT SHORT AND SWEET

- RESIST TRYING TO MAKE SENSE OF IT

- DON'T DESCRIBE IT TO YOURSELF OR
  TRY TO REACH CONCLUSIONS

- AVOID JUDGMENTS OR CRITIQUES

- JUST DO IT AND THEN THROW IT AWAY

- SIT AND MOVE ON. TOMORROW WILL BE A DIFFERENT EXPRIENCE
  (NOT NECESSARILY BETTER OR WORSE)

- LET YOUR MEMORY OF THE LAST MEDITATION GO

- EVERY TIME YOU SIT, ACT AS IF IT'S FOR THE FIRST TIME

- RESIST APPLAUSE (AND BOOING AND EVERYTHING ELSE)

- ALLOW YOURSELF TO BE SURPRISED

HOME AWAY

I was at a retreat last summer and meditated twice a day, every day. But since I have been home, I can't do it. Why?

Welcome to the retreat bubble. Within this safe and quiet place, there aren't any disruptions or background noises or excuses not to meditate (except those in your mind). Retreats are designed to make you show up. And voilà, most people show up and meditate and love it because there's nothing else to do.

NOTES FROM THE CUSHION

Our friend Petra started seeing a meditation teacher because of terrible insomnia due to a crappy divorce. Meditation cured her insomnia . . . but only when she meditated. Because she was convinced that she couldn't meditate on her own, on the nights she didn't see her teacher, she also didn't sleep. She's our poster girl for why a real, consistent, self-led practice can change and possibly save your life. And this is why it's essential to develop your own practice—and own it.

RELAX—JUST DO IT

THE TRAILBLAZER: HERBERT BENSON

Way back in the 1970s, there was a doctor from Harvard named Herbert Benson, who studied the connection between the mind and the body and stress and sickness. He discovered that you have to treat the mind in order to treat the body, and he came up with a tool to alleviate stress, which he called the relaxation response (aka meditation). What he found was that meditation is the antidote for the fight-or-flight state. In other words, it's kryptonite for stress.

MEDITATION IS NOT GOING TO MAKE YOU BORING AND UPTIGHT, BUT JUDGING SOMETHING YOU'VE NEVER DONE BEFORE COULD DO JUST THAT.

LIKE A PRAYER

I'm a Christian. I understand prayer, but meditation seems a little out there for me.

Various forms of meditation exist within every major religion, including Christianity. There is nothing sacrilegious about meditation (unless perhaps you've come up with a really mean mantra about your next-door neighbor or something). If you pray, then you are already familiar with slowing down and focusing your mind. All the great mystics have been meditating for centuries, and if you start you will be in good company: Thomas Aquinas, Thomas Merton, Teresa de Ávila, Francis de Sales, Simone Weil, and Ignatius of Loyola, just to name a few.

WARNING SIGNS

Can it be dangerous?

Meditation is simply focusing on your breathing without judgment while seated in a comfortable position. It is only dangerous if you do it while driving or operating heavy machinery.

BELIEVE IT OR NOT

Do I have to believe in something like God or the universe for meditation to work?

The beauty of meditation is that there is no one way or one set of beliefs required to do it, and no penalties or appraisals for not doing it. But it does help to believe in yourself and in your ability to show up.

Can I do meditation wrong?

Nope. It might be unhelpful if you are too hard on yourself, tell yourself you suck, or not do it in the first place. Aside from all that, you can't really mess it up.

How can I know what type of meditation I should do?

There are oh-so-many paths and types and techniques, so try any or all and see what catches your fancy. You can do breath work until you pass out; listen to guided meditations or the songs of whales in Fiji or the ringing of Tibetan singing bowls in the Himalayas; you can sing kirtan until your throat is sore or repeat mantras until you are fluent in Sanskrit or listen to dharma talks until you've filled the void. The most important thing, the only thing that matters, is that you meditate.

NOTES FROM THE CUSHION

Sukey experimented for eons before settling on a preferred method. She loves props—she used to bring a second suitcase full of bells and gongs and gold bowls to meditation retreats. She wanted to make her meditation "sacred." But times have changed; because of Elizabeth's Spartan tendencies and her continuous influence, Sukey can now meditate anywhere, anytime, with no props, no cushion, no Palo Santo. After meditating for a long time, she started to see that she didn't need props; everything—including fluorescent lighting, ambulance sirens, and shag carpeting—is already sacred.

Which technique is best for a beginner?

Start. That's the best technique. Just sit today—not tomorrow or next week or when your kids go off to college. We recommend starting with the simplest and most basic technique: counting your breath. It doesn't sound exciting, but that's sort of the point. When your mind wanders or wonders—and it will—just come back to your breath and begin to count again.

MAKE IT A HABIT

There was a time when people didn't brush their teeth often—or at all. This is true. It just wasn't a thing.

In fact, toothbrushing didn't become widespread in the United States until after World War II. At first, dental hygienists tried to spread the word through the grown-up grapevine, telling people that they could avoid the fate of growing old and toothless by brushing regularly. But, for some reason, it didn't catch on, and people's teeth kept falling out. Then those same dental hygienists came up with Plan B: They went into the schools and taught the kids to brush.

Lo and behold, the practice stuck; unlike their parents, the kids didn't have settled hygiene habits (or lack thereof), and so they picked it up without a hitch. Soon that poor generation of adults who didn't listen to the hygienists were spending their golden years slurping soups and drinking their dinners. Meanwhile, that younger, fresh-breathed, and fully toothed generation had grown up and passed the habit on to their own kids.

Why are we telling you this sad but true story? Because meditation is a habit, too.

CHAPTER 2

WHY AREN'T YOU MEDITATING?

THE MANY WAYS THAT MEDITATION WILL FIX UP YOUR LIFE

You want better health, less stress, less worry, less anxiety, less depression, less fear, less sickness, less exhaustion, less anger, less delusion, less dependency on booze, drugs, food, cigarettes, and someone else's love.

You want more reality, more joy, more feeling, more energy, more connection, more vibrancy, more passion, more clarity, more freedom, and way more love.

By now most people are aware of the many benefits of meditation, but for some mysterious reason they still don't meditate. As perplexing as that may sound, it is a known fact that we humans often do not do what will help or even save us.

A good question to ask yourself: What brings you here? Why do you want to meditate? For some of you the answer might be obvious: you are in the middle of a major crisis or on the verge of a nervous breakdown or at the end of your rope. You guys don't even need to read the rest of this chapter. Go ahead and skip to chapter 3. You don't need to hear the long list of benefits that will help you to show up and sit every day. All that pain is enough of a catalyst for change.

As for the rest of you, those of you who might be experiencing some low-grade suffering but are by no means in acute pain, a little motivation goes a long way. Trust us, it will get you to the cushion. The best part about motivators when it comes to meditation is that there are so many to choose from. Face it, all of us could use a little soul searching; even the perfect girl from high school is all grown up and falling apart on the inside. Trust us.

So take a little inventory.

FIND A GOOD REASON TO GET STARTED.

THE MANY FACES OF MEDITATION

ANXIETY KILLER

Meditation spotlights where your inner unrest begins and what triggers your mind and its spin, so that you can observe: the voices, the stories, the thoughts that nag, berate, belittle, worry, warn, judge, you know, *those* voices—the critics and the award-givers.

ANTINUMBING AGENT

To wake you up so that you don't tranquilize yourself with booze, medication, food, TV, Facebook, or whatever your addiction of choice is. Meditation teaches you to self-soothe so that you don't rely on a bunch of unhelpful externals.

INNER CHEERLEADER

To bring you out of your funk and into the world, to fight the good fight (you versus whatever ails you). Meditation is a personal support system, like a pep rally for one.

MEDICINE MAN

To heal your stress-ravaged body. Meditation is the counteragent for a fight-or-flight response. It lowers cortisol, blood pressure, and the heart rate, and is anti-inflammatory. Inflammation is the root of all disease: heart disease, cancer, and dementia to name a few.

BRAIN TRAINER

Studies show that brand-new meditators can grow more gray matter in their brain in as little as 20 minutes a day for 8 weeks. You will see changes in memory, empathy, and stress levels. Who doesn't want that?

ON-CALL THERAPIST

To feel your feelings (for real), to be in your life, to work on your wounds, and to finally deal with your shit.

LIFEGUARD

To save you from your own bad choices. Meditation shines the light on you and why you do what you do so that you have some time to think about it before you do it again.

SANDMAN

To sleep through the night. Studies show that meditation is better than a sleeping pill for getting to sleep, staying asleep, and waking up with good energy. Plus, there's no hangover.

DNA REPAIRPERSON

To take charge of your DNA and impact the way that your genes express themselves as you age. Start meditating to push the first symptoms of any inherited disease so far away in the future that you never experience them in your lifetime.

MAGICIAN

To see that it is all a choice. That nothing is good or bad, it simply is what it is. The magician will show you the blessings in every situation, no matter what.

ELEVATE YOUR MIND: PHYSICAL BENEFITS

STRESS AWARDS

We talk about stress like it's a badge of honor when in fact it's a real killer. We all buy into this crazy lie that somehow stress helps us, that it keeps us productive. We love to brag about it: I'm so tired, so stressed; I worked 98 hours this week; I'm a doer, look at me. As if running ourselves into the ground is a recipe for success, when in reality it's not that cool. What are we doing? Why are we in collective denial over this?

We all know that 95% of diseases are either caused by or worsened by stress. So why do we wait for the heart attack, the cancer diagnosis, the stroke, before we take stress seriously? Because we're conditioned to ignore it, to be productive, to overextend, to say yes to too many things, to say no to sleep, self-care, down time, and connection, and to feel guilty for wanting those things or actually feeling like we deserve them.

We resist connection, even a connection to our own bodies. Stress makes everything harder, more chaotic, and crazier, and because of that, you get less done, less effectively, and less efficiently.

NOTES FROM THE CUSHION

Sukey's mother has early-onset Alzheimer's. Symptoms began when she was only in her 50s. Fearing that she could inherit the disease, Sukey paid a visit to a specialist, who informed her that her genes didn't have to be her destiny, but without a proper diet, exercise, and a daily meditation program they probably were.

DOCTOR'S ORDERS

Doctors are recommending a daily meditation practice for health and longevity. It turns out that meditation ranks up there with quitting smoking, eating well, and working out. In fact, it might be the most important of all the changes, because not only does meditation reduce stress and lower blood pressure, but it will also give you the discipline to change your diet, ease off the drinking or smoking, and start going to the gym.

Meditation creates awareness and slows you down so that it'll be far easier to choose a salad over a cupcake or a seltzer over a shot of tequila. And since you won't be in a food coma or have a horrid hangover, chances are you'll make it to the gym. So, yeah–listen to your doctor, meditate.

10 MILLION AMERICANS MEDITATE, 6 MILLION OF THEM BECAUSE THEIR DOCTORS TOLD THEM TO

DISCONNECT

Our bodies don't lie. They live in reality, which makes them wonderful barometers for our stress levels. Have you recently gained a ton of weight? Or lost your appetite completely? Are you coming down with the flu every other week? Do you look like an old hag? Are you exhausted even when you first wake up? Or, do you not fall asleep in the first place? Is your sex drive parked? How about headaches? Backaches? Earaches? Neck aches?

These are the warning signs that often appear before the big cosmic slaps. Pay attention to your body, it knows a great deal more than you do. Your body will let you know when you're out of balance and when stress is taking over, and it often gives you an opportunity to do something about it before it becomes the big C, your ticker gives out, or something even worse. The problem is that most of us don't take these warning signs seriously; we push through and ignore them until it's too late.

SADLY, STRESS IS THE NEW NORMAL

Our bodies are in a constant fight-or-flight mode, as if we are in the midst of escaping from prison, being chased by bloodhounds, when in reality we are at the office getting reprimanded by the boss for coming in late.

It's not healthy or fun to walk around like your pants are on fire. So what can we do about it? Meditate. The reason that meditation reduces stress is because the deep breathing activates your parasympathetic nervous system and meditation focuses the mind on the mantra and off the chatter or the story that is typically amplifying the stress to begin with. So, like we have been saying, just sit.

BUT, REMEMBER, MEDITATION IS A LIFELONG THING

You can bring down your blood pressure by meditating for a couple of months, but if you want to keep it down, then you need to keep sitting.

Why are we depressing you with this information? Because we have a solution: Meditate.

PRIMATE PROBLEMS

THE PROFESSOR: ROBERT SAPOLSKY

Robert Sapolsky, neuroscientist, primatologist, writer, and professor at Stanford University, has spent decades studying stress and how it affects both humans and baboons. He will tell you that prolonged stress will make you physically and physiologically sick and that being the low man or monkey on the totem pole is a big factor in stress and stress-related illness. Any kind of stress keeps us in fight-or-flight mode, and if fight-or-flight is turned on for too long, we get sick. And sometimes we die.

CRYING WOLF

Our bodies can't tell the difference between the fight-or-flight mode that comes from real live danger, like sharks or ghosts, and the fight-or-flight mode that comes from daily stress like paying bills or angry spouses. To make matters worse, our minds don't even know that we are in fight-or-flight in the first place.

Do you get tension headaches before a work assignment is due? Does commuting make you sweat—even in the winter? Do you suffer from insomnia? Is your best friend a cigarette? Are you eating your emotions? If you answered yes to any of these questions, you are probably stuck in fight-or-flight, or at least spend a lot of time there.

Being aware that you are in fight-or-flight is the first step to getting out.

Then what? you may ask. Well, let us introduce you to the magical mind-body connector that can make all of your dreams come true, or at least keep you out of constant fight-or-flight. So without further ado, let us introduce you to **THE VAGUS!**

THE VAGABOND

The vagus is the longest nerve in the body. It runs from deep within the brain, through the heart, and into the gut. It's been called the connector, the wanderer, the vagabond, or the compassion nerve. It controls breathing, digestion, and heart rate, as well as our reactions and responses, and can act as a brake pedal for fight-or-flight.

Meditation and deep breath work give the vagus a workout so that when you go into fight-or-flight mode you don't get hijacked by it. The better your vagal tone (the more you activate the vagus), the better your ability to slow down and observe what the situation actually requires of you, instead of throwing yourself into "I'm about to be killed by a tiger" mode.

Meditating will help you develop a healthy resilient vagal tone, which can be measured by heart variability, which is indicated by an increase of heart rate when you inhale and a decrease of heart rate when you exhale.

High stress, a lack of sleep, and long work weeks are a few of the things that make your vagal tone drop. What can you do to increase it? It sounds a little creepy, but it's not—we swear, you can stimulate it. How? No, not like that . . .

WAYS TO STIMULATE THE VAGUS
YEAH, THAT'S A THING

Tea party:
Immerse your face in icy water for as long as you can stand it.

Humming:
Humming lowers cortisol levels and chills you out.

Hugging:
Who doesn't like a hug?

Exercise:
Run, swim, jump—just move.

Singing:
Whether you are in the shower, at karaoke, or in the rain, singing activates the vagus. So croon away.

Dancing:
Shake it like you just don't care.

Breathe:
All breath work is great for stimulating the vagus.

Being kind:
Go do something for someone else. It's a helpful way to get over yourself.

AN OLDIE BUT A GOODIE

One of our favorite types of breath work is Breath of Fire. It's been stimulating vagus nerves for thousands of years. It's also known as kapalabhati, the cleaning breath. It's like Roto-Rooter for the body: it detoxes the lungs, helps with respiratory problems, increases circulation, strengthens the nervous system (vagus), increases endurance, clears the mind, stimulates energy flow, reboots the muscles, and strengthens the abs.

BREATH OF FIRE

1. TAKE A SEAT

Sit in the same posture you use for meditation.
Or, if you'd rather, sit in a squat. But sit tall with a straight spine.

2. BEGIN

Take a few deep belly breaths.

3. BREATHE

Inhale deeply and exhale forceful, short, quick breaths from your nose (really forceful—so much so that you activate your navel).

4. START WITH ONE MINUTE

Some Breath of Fire experts can go for 11 or 12 minutes. Life goals . . .

SANE PAIN

75% OF AMERICAN ADULTS LIVE WITH CHRONIC PAIN

Oxycodone and morphine are the go-to painkillers for American doctors. They work in the moment but for long-term use, they've wrecked a lot of lives. Opiates are risky, addictive, and often soul destroying. The truth is, meditation will not kill pain like an opiate will (obviously), but it is incredibly helpful in pain management because it reduces the pain's intensity by distracting the brain from buying into the pain in the first place.

POSTOP

The number one postsurgery risk is infection. An infection won't just slow the healing down—it will destroy the entire process. It might sound crazy to you non-believers, but meditation fights infection. How? you ask. When you meditate you lower your cortisol level, aka stress, which allows your body to multiply its white blood cells, and hence, fight the infection.

NiGHTY-NiGHT

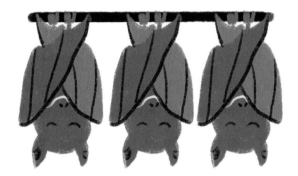

Sleeping pills are yet another crappy addiction that has invaded the Western world. Not only do they cause a hangover, which makes us feel horrible yet want more the next night, but they also have a tendency to make people slow and stupid . . . sounds like a shitty and unnecessary cycle to us, especially when we can just meditate instead. Meditation helps with sleep disorders because it does a good job of taking away that sense of urgency—you are not going to solve the world's problems at 2:30 a.m., nor will you solve most of your own.

Meditation helps settle the brain's nervous system—like a good massage or a warm cup of milk.

MEDITATION HELPS US SNOOZE IN TWO WAYS:

LONG-TERM EFFECTS: A daily meditation practice slows the nervous system, decreases anxiety, and makes it a whole lot easier to fall asleep.

SHORT-TERM EFFECTS: As in right this very moment when you desperately want to fall asleep—meditation will help you to focus on the breath to take your mind away from the spin. It will make you relax and hopefully soothe you to sleep.

COUNTING SHEEP MEDITATION

1. CLOSE YOUR EYES AND LIE THERE (but read the rest of the instructions before you do).

2. PLACE YOUR HANDS on your stomach so that you can feel your breath.

3. IMAGINE the cutest baby lamb you've ever seen. He is about 10 yards from a stone wall. There's a lush green pasture on the other side of the wall.

4. BREATHE in a deep belly breath and watch the tiny lamb run toward the wall.

5. AS THE TINY LAMB JUMPS over the wall, breathe out, and count 1.

6. OH, LOOK, there's his brother—over there on the other side of the wall. Repeat steps 4 and 5 and count 2.

7. REPEAT until you are counting Zs instead of sheep.

BETTER THAN BOTOX

Let's do a little test. Go to the mirror and make the tightest, hardest pinched face that you can. Take a real look. This is standing stress face (often confused with its cousin standing bitch face). In some ways, your mother was right—if you make a certain face long enough, it will stick. So if things don't change, this is your future look.

Ah, but as always, you have a choice. Stay this way or take 20 minutes every day and meditate. What will that do for your furrowed brow, you might ask? It will slowly soften as you let go of all the stress and tension in that gorgeous face. Even if the lines stay, they're no longer active, meaning they add grace without strain.

BABY FACE

THE DISCOVERER: ELIZABETH BLACKBURN

Elizabeth Blackburn won the Nobel Prize for the discovery of telomeres, which gave the scientific world the ability to measure aging and disease risk by looking at the telomeres. Telomeres are the caps on the ends of your chromosomes (like the plastic things on the end of shoelaces). They prevent the chromosomes from unraveling, which affects how quickly our cells age.

Blackburn knew that stress caused them to shorten, so she connected the dots and did a study on meditation—would it lengthen them? Yes, and apparently it works faster than a well-watered Chia Pet. In other words, she found the fountain of youth. Sorry, Ponce.

BENJAMIN BUTTON SYNDROME

Nothing ages a person more than stress. Just look at each president's pictures from before and after their time in office. Meditation not only lessens stress, but it also increases the length of our telomeres.

People with shorter telomeres are at greater risk for obesity, diabetes, heart disease, depression, the list goes on, and they die younger. So if anyone asks what you're doing when you are meditating, tell them you are growing out your telomeres.

PLASTIC FANTASTIC

The brain has plasticity, meaning it has the ability to change. Research proves that a regular meditation practice can cause the brain's cerebral cortex to thicken and grow by increasing the blood vessels and blood flow. The outer cortex runs the brain's learning and memory department. The actual practice of meditation grows the area of the brain that controls memory, concentration, attention, empathy, and self-control. It works in the same way that playing music grows the area of the brain associated with musical ability. Practice makes perfect.

LIGHT MY FIRE

If you are feeling old and worn-out for no reason, and your light has dimmed and your spark has faded, we have something very important to tell you: Nothing external is going to turn that shit back on. But meditation can help. It will allow you to become friends with yourself, to develop love and compassion and curiosity for you, which will give you the spark you need. We promise, sit for a few weeks, and in no time you'll have your shine back.

TRAIN YOUR BRAIN; OTHERWISE IT'S GOING TO ATROPHY LIKE EVERYTHING ELSE.

THIS IS YOUR BRAIN ON MEDITATION

PREFRONTAL CORTEX
STOP BINGE EATING,
DRINKING, SMOKING

HIPPOCAMPUS
WIN A SPELLING BEE, FIND
YOUR WAY IN THE WOODS,
REMEMBER PEOPLE'S NAMES

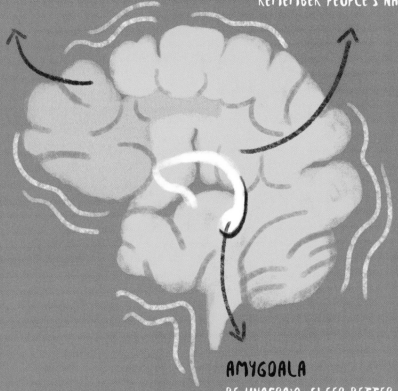

AMYGDALA
BE UNAFRAID, SLEEP BETTER,
STRESS LESS

PHYSICAL BENEFITS OF MEDITATION

LESSENS HEADACHES AND MIGRAINES

SOOTHES PSORIASIS

REDUCES ALLERGIES

REDUCES PMS

REDUCES HEART ATTACKS
AND STROKES

IMPROVES IMMUNE SYSTEM

INCREASES LONGEVITY

REDUCES INFECTION

REDUCES CHOLESTEROL LEVELS

HELPS POSTOPERATIVE HEALING

SOOTHES ARTHRITIS

REDUCES CHRONIC PAIN

INCREASES SKIN RESISTANCE

SLOWS AGING PROCESS

DECREASES HOSPITALIZATIONS

RELAXES NERVOUS SYSTEM

ALLOWS FOR RECOVERY FROM STRESS

RELIEVES INSOMNIA

IMPROVES SYMPTOMS OF ADHD

DECREASES HEART RATE

AIDS WITH WEIGHT LOSS

REDUCES INTENSITY OF PAIN

LOWERS BLOOD PRESSURE

REDUCES FREE RADICALS

IMPROVES FERTILITY

RELIEVES IMPOTENCE

IMPROVES CIRCULATION

INCREASES MUSCLE RELAXATION

INCREASES DHEA LEVELS

REDUCES BLOOD SUGAR LEVELS

ARE YOU CONVINCED YET? JUST SIT. NO MATTER WHAT.

MANAGING DISCOMFORT IS THE SINGLE MOST IMPORTANT SKILL FOR THE 21ST CENTURY.

DR. MARC SCHOEN

MEDITATION

Everyone's talking about it. It'll make you feel good. It gives you clarity. Takes you out of your head. Relaxes you. Grounds you. It's like a mother's hug. It softens the edges, reduces the noise, and takes the bigness out of the not-so-big things. It soothes the soul; it connects you to your inner voice, your center, your aliveness, your intuition, your real voice of reason. Sit with yourself now. This is the big stuff: Sitting, no matter how uncomfortable you are, and getting to know yourself, is the key to being in your life and to a better life. Way better.

MOOD SWINGS

MEDITATION TURNS FROWNS UPSIDE DOWN

The best way to instantly snap out of a low-grade anxiety attack or a dour, sour mood is to change your state. Stop. Breathe. Sit and meditate and release that crappy malaise and smile. Yes, force a huge grin while you meditate, as goofy as it feels, breathe in and say "smile" and breathe out and actually smile. Repeat until that smile is real.

PINS AND NEEDLES

Look, it's a very human experience to wake up and wonder, is this really it? How did I get here? But if you don't allow yourself to get hijacked by those thoughts and instead use the moment as an opportunity for growth, then it can be a real blessing. Meditation is what turns curses into blessings. So before you blow up your life: Observe, observe, observe.

Meditation will help you sit with those uncomfortable feelings that you're having, which in turn will hopefully give you the emotional strength to have difficult conversations with people in your life. Meditation can also help with clarity, perspective, and getting out of emotional conflict.

So just sit, no matter what.

MEDITATION IS A DIRECT LINE TO YOUR VOICE OF REASON.

BURNiNG OOWN THE HOUSE

Meditation will help you quit booze, smoking, cocaine, crack, meth, heroin, toxic relationships, terrible jobs, gambling, online shopping addictions, social media obsessions, a bad french fry habit, or any other black hole you can think of. Why? Because meditation teaches you how to fill your own black holes—so that you don't need any of the above-mentioned crap in your body or your life. And because it shines a light on WTF you are doing to yourself in the first place.

MEOiTATiON TEA(HES YOU TO SELF-SOOTHE.

NOTES FROM THE (USHiON

Elizabeth smoked a pack and a half of cigarettes a day for more than 20 years. When she decided that enough was enough, she smoked her last cigarette and threw the rest away. She had never been able to quit for more than a few hours, but meditation changed the whole game. It made stopping doable, and she hasn't had a cigarette since.

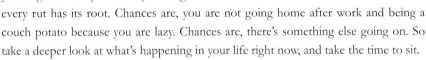

RUTS AND ROOTS

Meditation is a supertool for becoming unstuck. It will help you to get out of your rut by finding the root cause—and every rut has its root. Chances are, you are not going home after work and being a couch potato because you are lazy. Chances are, there's something else going on. So take a deeper look at what's happening in your life right now, and take the time to sit.

DELAY NO MORE

If you have a difficult time starting anything, try meditating first. Meditation is an elixir for procrastination. We avoid things because we don't enjoy being uncomfortable; we don't even enjoy made-up, illusory discomfort—that fear of things that might make us uncomfortable—so therefore we do anything possible not to do them. Meditation is a lifelong lesson in dancing with discomfort. It will give you the skills and ability to welcome that shit in every other aspect of your life—even the tough conversations, doing your taxes, writing that novel, or quitting the job you can't stand.

BRING IT ON

Meditation gives you the ability to take everything in—the good, the bad, and the ugly—and soon you'll realize that all of it is good, even the hardest parts. Meditation takes you from fear to love; most fear is imagined, and meditation takes us from the fear to the reality. It gives us the ability to differentiate the paper tiger from the real one, and teaches us not to be so afraid. When we learn to sit with fear, the fear loses its power. That is how to build courage.

MEDITATION WILL HELP YOU FIND YOUR INNER BADASS.

FEED YOUR HEAD

Meditation loves to give us all sorts of unexpected perks and gifts, like increased mental strength, focus, and creativity. The awareness that goes hand-in-hand with a medidation practice will seep into every aspect of your life. It's a superpower. Ask any creative soul who meditates; having a practice feeds the head and gives us access to a whole new realm of creative ideas and solutions. Meaning, aside from helping the artists and the professionals tap into their inner flow, meditation will make you a better letter writer, breakfast chef, adventure photographer, Halloween costume maker, birthday cake confectioner, craft cocktail maker, face painter, karaoke singer, interpretive dancer, or pet groomer; it will even assist you in the garden. Meditation helps you to take the risk to be vulnerable, to build the courage required for authentic self-expression, and it aids in developing the tolerance to handle criticism. So sit, and then go make something beautiful.

DO ONE THING MOST

Multitasking is for suckers. A long time ago someone started a rumor that women were really good multitaskers, and although it's true, it's not helpful. Many of us fell for the flattery, and we ran with it to the point where we are capable of doing 19 things at the same time. We often even look down on less versatile taskers. Let that shit go right now.

No one ever did anything better when they were doing 3 other things at the same time. So, instead, try doing one thing most, whether it's washing the dishes, driving the car, listening to your BFF's heartbreak, playing UNO with your kids, writing a scathing email, working on your tan, or doing side sit-ups. Meditation is a practice of doing one thing most, so start there and let it grow.

EMOTIONAL BENNIES OF MEDITATION

IMPROVES SELF-AWARENESS

INCREASES FEELINGS OF HAPPINESS

ALLOWS US TO SIT WITH PARADOX

INCREASES KINDNESS, TRUST, PATIENCE, AND ACCEPTANCE

ALLOWS US TO GIVE FEARS A NAME

REDUCES EMOTIONAL EATING

DECREASES LONELINESS

HELPS WITH FEELING LESS THAN OR NOT ENOUGH OR UNLOVABLE

REVEALS OUR SHADOW SIDE

INCREASES SELF-ESTEEM

SHINES A LIGHT ON CONFLICT

DECREASES DEPRESSION

HELPS WITH PARENTING

INCREASES MOTIVATION

HELPS WITH ADDICTION

INCREASES COMPASSION

DECREASES WORRY

DECREASES ANXIETY

IMPROVES MOOD

ALLOWS FOR FREEDOM

GIVES MENTAL TOUGHNESS

COMPLEMENTS THERAPY

TEACHES US TO EMBRACE WHAT IS

ALLOWS US TO CONFRONT SHAME

UNCOVERS CONDITIONING

BUILDS MENTAL TOUGHNESS

REDUCES REACTIVITY

GETS US IN TOUCH WITH OUR INTUITION

HELPS WITH MENTAL STRENGTH AND INTELLIGENCE

IMPROVES DECISION MAKING

MEDITATION shines a light on fears and allows us to sit with them: fear of memories, fear of who we are, who we might become, of being well, of losing crutches, of sitting with the self; fear of the mystery, of our own darkness, of what we put in your own basements, attics, of lurking thoughts and repressed memories; fear that somehow if we go there we might fall apart, that we might unravel, that we might turn into someone else; fear of who that person is, might be; fear of change because there is a huge safety in not changing even if we feel terrible . . .

IF YOU WANT YOUR LIFE TO LOOK DRASTICALLY DIFFERENT, THEN YOU HAVE TO DO IT DRASTICALLY DIFFERENTLY.

CHAPTER 3

JUST SIT, NO MATTER WHAT

FOR MEDITATION TO WORK, YOU ACTUALLY HAVE DO IT

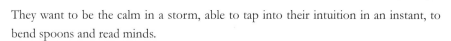

It's that simple. Everyone loves the idea of meditation, of seeing themselves on top of the mountain, eyes closed, sun setting, enlightenment coursing through their veins.

They want to be the calm in a storm, able to tap into their intuition in an instant, to bend spoons and read minds.

Even though most of us are well aware of the endless list of benefits, we still avoid sitting and meditating. Why? Why is meditation so difficult to start? In part, because we don't feel like we are doing anything. Cleaning old makeup brushes can feel more productive than sitting in meditation sometimes can.

The biggest secret to meditation is all you need to do is show up. You don't have to be good at it. You don't even need to know you are doing it right. You only have to show up. Every day. That's it. The rest will come.

"I am not a meditator" is an extremely limiting belief. Sadly, that pitiful little belief is what keeps most people from ever trying it in the first place. So, from this point on, just own it . . . you are a meditator.

AND A MEDITATOR MEDITATES

REDEFINE YOUR LABELS

I'm not a public speaker, I'm not a runner, I'm not a water person, I'm not an extrovert, I'm not a writer, I'm not athletic, I'm not the marrying kind, I'm not a kid person. There are thousands of disclaimers to choose from—and each of us has 5 or 55 that we rely on. Think about yours. Where do they come from? Are they even true or have you been telling yourself these stories for so long that you now believe your own press? Take one—whether it's "I'm not a runner" or "I'm not a writer"—and change it right now. Go for a small jog or write a letter and start becoming these things. Anyone can become most of the things they label themselves unable to be.

These stories become our unhealthy habits and addictions and then our identities. Someone whose story has always been "I'm not athletic" is very unlikely to start working out. The story prolongs the suffering. The same goes for the alcoholics who tell themselves that their role in life is being the life of the party, and they stay drunk and unhappy instead of looking at the thousands of other parts that make them human. This shit is powerful and controlling and we fall for it every single day. We create our cages. One of meditation's many, many gifts is the awareness that allows us to drop the story.

WARNING: CONDITIONING IMPAIRS FREEDOM

BACKGROUND: Domesticated elephants are trained when they are young and weak. They are tethered to trees with ropes or chains so that they won't roam or run away. They often try to break free but aren't yet strong enough to do so. As they get older and stronger—strong enough to uproot huge trees and snap any rope or chain—they become more than capable of breaking free, but because of their conditioning they no longer try. They can be tied up with a skinny little string and it's enough.

OUTCOME: That is how conditioning works. So much of what we were told or taught as kids has stayed true—you're not enough, you can't do it, you suck—and this is where limitations are born and can stay with us for a lifetime. This is learned helplessness. So if you want to stay shackled and limited, then don't meditate. But if you want to be free, really free from old stories and faulty conditioning, then start with meditation.

LiMiTiNG STORiES ABOUT MEDiTATiON

MYTH

REALiTY

Meditation is religious and cultish.

Meditation is about you getting to know you, finding your inner peace and goodness, and falling in love with the whole world. There's no need to go to the ashram or shave your head (unless you want to).

If I meditate too much, I will lose my edge and my creativity. I need my demons.

Then sit down and get to know your demons. Observe them; they probably have a lot to teach you.

Meditation is selfish.

Meditation makes you nicer, and people will like you better.

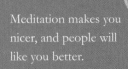

Meditation will make me lose my drive for success.

Meditation will help you to focus on what's actually important so that you can get shit done.

To get anything out of it, you need to meditate for hours.

Even a few minutes a day will change your life.

i WANT TO MEDITATE BUT . . .

i DON'T HAVE THE TIME

DOWNTIME: You can find 20 minutes. Wake up a little earlier; go to bed a little later. Take a break at the office and shut your door and close your eyes. Or sit in your car before you go in. What about the wasted Internet time, TMZ, shopping, nonsense news? There's an extra 20 minutes in there somewhere. We all waste a lot more time than that each day, no matter how busy we are.

SLOW THE CLOCK: Meditation slows the spin that's ever present in our minds and shows us the amazing amounts of time that we waste worrying, obsessing, listing, reliving, plotting, revenging, wishing, and dreading. When those little nuisances get pushed out of the way, all sorts of time slips in through the back door. It's an investment.

NOTES FROM THE CUSHION

We start every day at our office with a 20-minute meditation. That way we are sure to get it in. It's always nicer to do it together and it sets the tone for the day.

i'm worried that i'll end up passive and lazy

Meditation is about sitting with yourself, all the parts of you including your discomfort, your fears, your anxieties, your demons, and your ghosts. And just sitting with them, but not judging them, not criticizing, not categorizing, not justifying, not hiding, not running from them or ducking out. It's as far away from lazy as you can get; in fact, it's tremendously challenging, but in order to understand that, you actually have to do it. Meditation is the opposite of passive.

i don't want to become self-absorbed

Meditation is about becoming friends with yourself, which allows you to own (and love) all parts of yourself: the good, the bad, and the downright unsightly. Once you stop judging and begin accepting yourself, then meditation stops being about you. But we mean ALL the parts of yourself—not just the cute ones; you know, the parts of you that you pretend don't exist: jealousy, superiority, meanness . . . This will allow you to develop a deeper level of compassion for yourself. Soon you will see others through that same lens. The reality is that sitting for 20 minutes a day is indeed about you, but through that process you will become more giving, kinder, and more compassionate during the other 23 hours and 40 minutes a day.

i WORRY THAT MEDITATION WILL FEED MY OBSESSIVE THINKING

Ruminating, or stewing, or rehashing is what a lot of people do when they meditate and then they breathe and focus on the breath for 3 seconds until they're stewing again. That is the nature of the practice. If you sit consistently, you'll start to ruminate less and observe more, and you will notice that deep breathing or focusing on your breath or a mantra will pull you out of the rumination, aka the stew.

iF i HAVE AN EXTRA 20 MINUTES i'D RATHER WORK OUT

Wait, this does not need to be an either/or scenario. We bet you can find time for both. No matter how busy you are, if you make something a priority, time will open up in your life. But if you limit yourself and your time, you'll notice that you don't have much. There will be a lot of things you'll have less time for: love, connection, work, family, friends, vacation, fun, and wonder.

i CAN'T GET STARTED

As long as you are actually trying, you can't meditate incorrectly. So let that go. There's no wrong way to do it, as long as it's just you and your breath. So when you hear the voice of your inner bully pushing you around, don't fall for it. Observe it and move on.

TOUGH GUY

THE MASTER: BRUCE LEE

Bruce Lee, the Hong Kong martial artist, actor, philosopher, filmmaker, poet, founder of Jeet Kune Do, and all-around legend, is probably the most iconic image there is when it comes to discipline. He was known to do a thousand sit-ups and push-ups every day. He never stopped moving, except in meditation. He trained his mind as much as his body.

WHY AREN'T YOU MEDITATING?

NONHELPFUL STORY	HELPFUL STORY
I'm not a meditator.	I wanna be like Bruce Lee.
I suck at this; my mind won't shut up.	I wanna be like Bruce Lee.
I'm way too busy to actually meditate.	I wanna be like Bruce Lee.
It feels selfish.	I wanna be like Bruce Lee.
I need to deal with reality.	I wanna be like Bruce Lee.
Meditation is too hard.	I wanna be like Bruce Lee.
It takes years to benefit from it.	I wanna be like Bruce Lee.
I'm too restless.	I wanna be like Bruce Lee.
It's not my thing.	I wanna be like Bruce Lee.

KEEP IT SIMPLE

Getting started is the most difficult step in developing any type of habit, not just meditation. Try starting small by gently asking yourself to take a deep breath every time your phone buzzes; or every time you get up from your desk chair; the next time you fill up your car, take 5 belly breaths as you pump gas.

MEDITATION ISN'T HARD

Learning astrophysics is hard. Doing aerial flips on a balance beam is hard. Winning the Tour de France is hard. Meditation is pretty easy. If you can breathe, you are halfway there. Of course, there are a few tricks to make it even easier: show up, show up, show up.

IF YOU WANT A BETTER LIFE, THEN BE BETTER AT SHOWING UP FOR IT.

DON'T BE A DOUBTING THOMAS

We are a results-oriented culture. We want numbers and data and proof. But not all aspects of meditation are tangible. You can't measure the results or benefits or changes in the same way that you can with diet and exercise. Yes, scientists and doctors are analyzing all sorts of physical results (and the studies are phenomenal), but unless you're going to get monthly MRIs and have your blood pressure checked on a daily basis, you probably won't be doing any measuring.

Instead you will notice that you've handled a situation completely differently from the way you have handled similar situations your entire life up until that point. Those types of results and benefits aren't very measurable, but they're really what meditation is all about.

MAKE iT STiCKY

1. One day at a time. Meditate today. That's it.

2. Pick a time each day and then pick somthing you already do, like brushing your teeth. For the next week after your choppers are cleaned, take 10 minutes, close your eyes, and focus on your breath. Do it twice a day if you can.

3. Keep going. If you miss a day, SO WHAT? Just start again.

BOOT CAMP

Discipline is something we develop. If you haven't been building it, you can't pull it out of your back pocket. That'd be like running a marathon when you haven't run around the block in 10 years. You might be able to do it, but it would suck, and chances are you wouldn't try it again. Instead, the next time it was required of you, you'd say, "Oh, me, no, I don't have that kind of discipline." Of course you don't. You have to do the work.

Until you make meditation a priority, there will always be something else you could be doing. So don't wait for all the doing to be done and all the lists to be checked off, because there is an endless supply of them. Discipline is all about showing up at the cushion even when you are tired, sick, grumpy, or just don't want to. Show up for any amount of time. Show up with any kind of attitude. Even if you show up and all you are thinking about is how you don't want to meditate today, just shut up and observe your negative thought loop.

MAKE iT DOABLE

JUST SiT FOR 8 WEEKS

Sometimes in life it's easier to have a plan. For a lot of people, 8 weeks seems to be a golden number, because it's enough time to get going **AND** feel some results. It's kind of like preseason for meditation practice. It's light and easy and most important, it's doable.

JUST SIT: 8 WEEKS TO BUILD A PRACTICE

WEEK 1
EVERY BREATH YOU TAKE
3 MINUTES A DAY

FOCUSING ON THE BREATH

Keep it simple. Close your eyes and focus on your breath. Inhale and exhale, and when your mind starts to wander, come back to the breath. Set your phone alarm for 3 minutes and stop when it goes off. Don't do more than that. This is training, not a competition (even with yourself).

HELPFUL HINT:

We suggest linking the time of day that you do this to something else that you already do. For instance, sit for 3 minutes while your coffee is brewing.

After sitting, take a moment to write down what you experienced or didn't experience in a notebook with the time and date. Sit for 7 days straight, but if you miss a day, start over at day 1 of week 1.

ONCE YOU REACH 7 DAYS IN A ROW, MOVE ON TO WEEK 2.

WEEK 2
ADD 'EM UP
4 MINUTES A DAY

COUNTING THE BREATHS

Slowly count to 4 as you inhale and slowly count to 4 as you exhale. With each count, touch your thumb to your pointer finger (1), then middle finger (2), then ring finger (3), and finally your pinkie (4). That's it. Then do it again and again. Your mind will wander, so start over when it does.

HELPFUL HINT:

Notice if you are rushing the count and slow it down. There's no finish line here.

After sitting, take a moment and write down what you experienced or didn't experience in a notebook with the time and date. Sit for 7 days straight, but if you miss a day, start over at day 1 of week 2.

ONCE YOU REACH 7 DAYS IN A ROW, MOVE ON TO WEEK 3.

WEEK 3
TRUST YOUR GUT
5 MINUTES A DAY

DEEP BELLY BREATHING

Place your hands on your stomach and as you breathe in, feel your stomach expand. As you breathe out, feel your stomach contract. Use your physical stomach as your anchor. When your mind wanders, let the feeling of your hands on your stomach bring you back to your breath.

HELPFUL HINT:

If you find this exercise uncomfortable, hold a small pillow against your stomach and use that as your anchor.

After sitting, take a moment and write down what you experienced or didn't experience in a notebook with the time and date. Sit for 7 days straight, but if you miss a day, start over at day 1 of week 3.

ONCE YOU REACH 7 DAYS IN A ROW, MOVE ON TO WEEK 4.

WEEK 4
TURN ON YOUR HEART LIGHT
6 MINUTES A DAY

HEART-OPENING MEDITATION

Sit comfortably and imagine a circle of light encompassing the space where your heart is. With each inhale, the light gets a tiny bit brighter, and with each exhale, it gets a tiny bit bigger, as if you are a living solar-energy panel. Do this for 6 minutes or until you need a stronger pair of sunglasses.

HELPFUL HINT:

Don't think so much about getting it right or think too much about what you are doing. Remember, you are just breathing.

After sitting, take a moment and write down what you experienced or didn't experience in a notebook with the time and date. Sit for 7 days straight, but if you miss a day, start over at day 1 of week 4.

ONCE YOU REACH 7 DAYS IN A ROW, MOVE ON TO WEEK 5.

WEEK 5
GOOD VIBRATIONS
8 MINUTES A DAY

MANTRA MEDITATION

Breathe in and gently say the word "Sat," and breathe out the word "Nam." Or "I am," or "Om Om," or "Your Mama," or any two words that work for you. The key with a mantra is that when you notice that you are no longer saying it, your mind has wandered and it's time to get back to saying the mantra.

HELPFUL HINT:

Find a word or words that resonate with you; you might have to try a few before finding one that works for you.

After sitting, take a moment and write down what you experienced or didn't experience in a notebook with the time and date. Sit for 7 days straight, but if you miss a day, start over at day 1 of week 5.

ONCE YOU REACH 7 DAYS IN A ROW, MOVE ON TO WEEK 6.

WEEK 6
SOUNDS OF SILENCE
10 MINUTES A DAY

DAILY SOUND MEDITATION

Listen to all of the sounds around you, even if you think there aren't any: sirens, traffic, city noise, the hum of the air conditioner, or your cat breathing. Quiet down and listen, really listen. When you feel your mind wandering, come back and listen to all the sounds around you. Observe with your ears. When you stop hearing things, you've drifted, so get back to the sounds.

HELPFUL HINT:

Focus on one sound.

After sitting, take a moment and write down what you experienced or didn't experience in a notebook with the time and date. Sit for 7 days straight, but if you miss a day, start over at day 1 of week 6.

ONCE YOU REACH 7 DAYS IN A ROW, MOVE ON TO WEEK 7.

WEEK 7
i CAN SEE CLEARLY NOW
15 MiNUTES A DAY

ViSUAL MEDiTATiON

Sit with your eyes open and focus on one object in the room. As you study said object, really pay attention to the details. When you notice that you are no longer focusing on it, that means your mind has wandered. Bring your attention back to the object.

HELPFUL HiNT:

We like to use flowers as the object for this meditation because nature never gets old.

After sitting, take a moment and write down what you experienced or didn't experience in a notebook with the time and date. Sit for 7 days straight, but if you miss a day, start over at day 1 of week 7.

ONCE YOU REACH 7 DAYS iN A ROW, MOVE ON TO WEEK 8.

WEEK 8
BRING IT ON
20 MINUTES A DAY

OPEN-AWARENESS MEDITATION

Sit and allow whatever comes up to come up: thoughts, sounds, smells, feelings, songs, yawns, poems, or knock-knock jokes.

Let whatever it is rise up and then let it go when you notice something else come in.

If your attention drifts, use any of the tools from weeks 1 through 7 to bring you back.

HELPFUL HINT:

We love the idea of a meditation buddy. That's why we meditate together. Consider asking a friend to join you in this endeavor. It makes it more fun and way easier to show up.

After sitting, take a moment and write down what you experienced or didn't experience in a notebook with the time and date. Sit for 7 days straight, but if you miss a day, start over at day 1 of week 8.

ONCE YOU REACH 7 DAYS IN A ROW:
CONGRATULATIONS! NOW YOU'VE GOT SKILLS. BRAVO!

EVEN IF THIS 8-WEEK PLAN TAKES YOU 18 WEEKS, IT'S A GREAT WAY TO GET A PRACTICE STARTED.

NOTES ON THE 8-WEEK PLAN

PRIME TIME

It's much easier to remember to sit if you make a plan to sit every morning the second your kids leave for school or after you feed your fish. So think of your reminder as if it's a kitchen timer going off. When the door slams shut behind the kiddies, *ding*—it's time to meditate. When the fish swim around nibbling on those little creepy fish flakes, *ding*, it's time to meditate.

JUST SIT

Most of us are all-or-nothing. So the idea of a meditation practice sparks an entire list of life-altering plans: quit drinking, quit smoking, stop eating so much, start exercising more, lose 30 pounds, go Paleo, do a digital detox, and get into therapy. Don't go changing everything at once—that kind of behavior belongs in the box with New Year's resolutions.

For these 8 weeks, simply focus on meditation. That is it. Just sit. Let's be real, you won't do any of the above if you try to do all of them at once—at least not for more than a day or two. Start with meditation and watch. Let it reveal what is causing you to pick up the cigarette, the doughnut, or that fifth glass of wine. Meditation will help you learn to be kind to yourself, and then it will be much easier to deal with all the self-destructive habits in your life.

DO IT ANYWAY

If it was easy to show up every day, everyone would do it. So whether you are too tired or sick or lazy, do it anyway. No one has ever said, "I regret meditating today."

GOOD THINGS COME TO THOSE WHO WAIT

A study from Washington University in St. Louis on delayed gratification showed that the better you feel about the future benefits of doing something challenging (like showing up for meditation), the more successful you will be at the challenging activity. Delaying gratification activates the prefrontal cortex. There is pleasure in knowing that good will come in the future from what you are doing or not doing right now.

The better you are at convincing yourself that meditation will bring you multiple benefits and change your life (and it will), the easier it will be to show up every day. The belief in the benefits can make the difference between meditating and not meditating. So don't stop believing.

POPULAR MEDITATION SPARK TIMES

 As soon as you get up in the morning

 Right after your first cup of coffee

 After walking the dog

 After you shower

 Before your workout

 After yoga

 Before work in your parked car

 During lunch

 After work in the driveway

 Before making dinner

 After putting the kids to bed

 Before you check your evening email

 After a glass of wine

 Before you go to sleep

⚠ ALERT: THERE IS NO INSTANT GRATIFICATION IN MEDITATION

Our addiction to instant gratification is a self-control problem. Just the small act of taking a breath, connecting, and becoming present slows you down and initiates a delay in the craving for instant gratification. That delay is the difference between responding and reacting, and it stops the autopilot loop of needing whatever it is that we think is going to soothe us in that moment. We are living in the age of "I want it now!"—with Seamless, Amazon, Netflix, Kindle, Uber, Twitter, Instagram, Facebook, texting, and Tinder. There is no wait time. The pleasure loop has a sneaky capacity to lull us into a stupor that makes us forget why we are buying or drinking or texting.

By observing these urges, we slow down and ask, Hey, why am I doing this?

BEFORE

AFTER

CHANGE STARTS WITH OBSERVING.

WATCH AND WAIT

- **WATCH:** Notice what is going on in your mind every time you have a craving.

- **WAIT:** Don't just go for it, meaning don't just order the shoes, grab the doughnut, check your email for the hundredth time. Wait—even if it's just for a few minutes and really pay attention to what you're doing.

SOME QUESTIONS YOU MIGHT ASK

NOT FAR NOW

How long does it take not to have to force yourself to show up to the cushion anymore, but to want to instead?

It takes as long as it takes. For some people it is immediate and for others an eternity. Chances are you'll be somewhere in between. The reality is that some days you will have to force yourself to the cushion and sometimes it will feel easy and natural. The key is not to worry too much about either experience. Notice whatever you may be feeling and sit anyway.

WHEN THE GOING GETS TOUGH

It's easy for me to schedule meditation time when life is smooth, but when stress takes over, I can't seem to do it.

That is normal and it's also why we practice. These stressful moments are exactly when you should be revving up your meditation practice. It's the best tool to pull out during tough times.

FAKE IT TILL YOU MAKE IT

What about the days when it feels fake and forced?

There definitely will be days when it will feel ridiculous or stupid or just plain awful—and those are as important or perhaps even more important than the days when it feels real and necessary. Even when you feel like a meditation fraud, sit. Everyone has those days. So what? Pay attention to what comes up. Let meditation serve as a spotlight as to what's going on in that crazy little brain of yours. Enjoy the show.

I seem to be getting worse at this, not better. When I started, 15 minutes wasn't a problem, and now I can barely last 5.

There's no worse or better. It's easy to sit for a longer period in the beginning because it's new and exciting. But you will have days when 5 minutes feels like 5 hours, and those might be the days when you need meditation the most. The key is to take all the rules and all the judgment out of the equation and just sit. Then come back tomorrow and do it again.

SO IF YOU THINK YOU DON'T HAVE AN EXTRA 20 MINUTES . . .

Gandhi had a lot on his plate, to say the least. While he was tossing the Brits out of India, steering his country toward independence, and fighting for equality for everyone, he still managed to walk at least 30 miles a day (30 miles as in 60,000 steps). So you'd probably understand if he said, "I don't have time to meditate." But he didn't, not even on a day that would push most humans over the edge. Instead, when asked, he said, "I have so much to accomplish today that I must meditate for two hours instead of one."

So stop whining and just sit.

CHAPTER 4

DIY MEDITATION: DO WHAT WORKS FOR YOU

HELPFUL AND NICE TO HAVE

You don't need anything aside from your attention to meditate. But for those of you who need a little more ritual in their ritual, we are here to suggest options when it comes to choosing where and when to sit every day, how to prepare your space, what to sit on, what to wear, whom to get help from, and what to expect from classes, workshops, and retreats.

You can take a bare-bones approach to your practice or find a space, create an altar, pull out that box of beads and malas from under your bed, douse yourself in essential oils, and burn some sage.

TIME AND SPACE

The beauty of meditation is that you can do it anywhere—on your couch, in your office, in prison, in church, at your kid's hockey game, at the DMV, on a chairlift, while getting your hair colored, during a pedicure, or in the sauna, the tub, the float tank, the Turkish bathhouse, or even midcolonic.

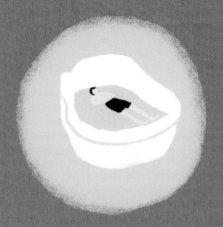

IT'S A PORTABLE TOOL

Once you have learned how to do it, you can do it anywhere. Look, there are no rules as to where and when to meditate, but there is power in meditating in the same place at the same time every day. Doing so serves as a reminder to show up, a reinforcement of sorts. It gets you in the mood, gives your practice weight, and adds magic to your life. And, hey—some people just like ritual.

So find a spot that works for you. It doesn't really matter where. If you can, come back to that place tomorrow and the day after. Let that place become your secret (or not-so-secret) meditation oasis, even if it's on the laundry room floor.

PRiME TiME

Some people might tell you that the really early hours are the best time for meditation because that's what takes place on many retreats and at many ashrams. But people also recommend walking on hot coals for conquering fears. We think it's a little silly to make something that is already hard to commit to even harder. Find a meditation time that works, a time when you will actually show up. If 3:45 a.m. is good for you, then rise and shine.

Don't make it special. Special creates a lot of expectations. Look at New Year's Eve: Everyone wants it to be the best night of their life and usually it's a complete shit show. Take the pressure off and show up for whatever time you have.

Even though there are no rules in meditation, a really good practice is to carve out space for it around another routine in your life. Meditate after you exercise, before you sauna, in the sauna, in the shower, after you feed the dog or the ferret or the Gila monster or the children (or whatever you have), or before your afternoon chardonnay or AA meeting.

FiNDiNG TiME iS NOT THAT TRiCKY

ASSUME THE POSiTiON

Even if you can't meditate for 5 minutes, sit cross-legged for 30 seconds before you fall asleep. By doing so, you are still showing up. If all else fails: Try again tomorrow.

MORNING, JOE

If you need coffee when you wake up, before you meditate, by all means have a cup of coffee, and then sit for 15 or 20 minutes. WARNING: This might not work for you if the caffeine revs you up too much. In that case, just have half a cup and drink the rest after. Enjoy your morning coffee and your morning meditation. Why can't they be friends?

MILESTONES

Big fat life moments like marriage, a partner moving in, a new baby, a promotion, or a move can all be routine killers. When things are good, it's easy to skip the sit and sip the champagne instead. Be vigilant, sit, and then toast to happy times.

ROAD TRIP

Create a space for meditation while traveling or it will be too easy to skip. As soon as you arrive and unpack, pick a meditation spot and time. And show up at the time and place each day and meditate.

NOTES FROM THE CUSHION

TRY THIS: Pull out the meditation cushion at night, in preparation for your morning sit. You'll go to sleep with the intention of meditating first thing, which helps keep the practice going.

HOTEL ROOMS HAVE MANY COZY LITTLE SPOTS FOR MEDITATION

Behind the curtain:

If you are looking for a cocoon to hide out in, just remember to face the window.

On the balcony:

If there is one, enjoy the great outdoors.

In the closet:

A great place to go if you are sharing the room.

In the chair:

Sit cross-legged or with your feet on the floor.

On the floor:

Use the bed to support your back.

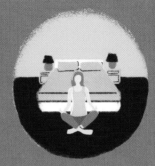

On the bed:

You can prop yourself up with pillows.

In the tub:

Feel free to use bubbles and a mask. We love a sitting soak.

On the toilet:

Really, it's great when traveling with kids. Go hide in the bathroom.

TAKE A SEAT

Some people love an altar, a teepee, a sweat lodge, a kiva, or a sage-infused sacred space, while others are fine meditating on their IKEA sofa. Either way, having a space that you feel good in will help you sit every day, and that's all that counts. You may find that once you start sitting, you'll want a specific spot to meditate in and you might even  want to add an altar with an incense burner or a set of Tibetan singing bowls. But do it because it makes sense to you, NOT because you think that having the props will make you a meditator; they won't.

FYI

If you fall asleep during meditation it does not have the same effect. That's called sleeping. (Maybe start a little earlier next time.)

iT ALL ADDS UP

More than anything else, we get asked how long a meditation session should last. Mostly because people want to know if a very short sit has any real effects. It all helps and the amount of time you sit isn't really that important. We like 20 minutes, but do what works for you. Something that both of us found helpful in the beginning was to start with small increments of time. The actual act of sitting is more important than how long you sit for.

MAKE IT A DOUBLE

If the commitment still scares you and need to break the amount of meditation time up and do a few small sits, then go ahead. Do whatever it takes. Later, you'll probably enjoy sitting for longer and you will definitely get more out of it. But when you are first starting out, don't add unnecessary pressure. Nothing is better or worse—just sit.

IF YOU BUILD IT, THEY WILL COME

Just like Kevin Costner, you, too, can create your own reality. You don't need to be an actor, either. You can simply picture yourself as a meditator, as someone who shows up to the same place at the same time every day and sits.

If you can picture that, then the chances are much greater that you will actually do it.

That goes for all sorts of things.

THE OFFICE

Many companies now have meditation or wellness rooms, or offer meditation classes or workshops at work. Even if yours doesn't, there are still many ways to sneak it in. If your boss has issues with it, explain to her that meditation helps with productivity, creativity, concentration, and focus, and gives the workspace a better vibe.

BELLS AND WHISTLES

An isolated cave might sound like the perfect place to meditate, but it's rarely an option, and you don't need to be in a quiet space anyway. Even if you work in a noisy, crowded office, there are ways to sit on the job. Plus, if you can meditate in a loud, chaotic space, it will help you keep your head on in your noisy everyday life.

PLACES TO MEDITATE AT THE OFFICE

 Bathroom: maybe not your first choice but whatever it takes.

 Put on your heaphones and fake it in front of your computer.

 Check the schedule for empty conference rooms.

 Do a quickie in the elevator.

 Stairwells everywhere have been empty ever since the smokers got kicked to the curb.

 Or skedaddle out of there and do a walking meditation.

OFFICE GETAWAYS

THE EXECUTIVE: JANICE MARTURANO

Janice Marturano, founder and executive director of the Institute for Mindful Leadership and a former VP at General Mills, is the meditation pioneer for corporate America. After going on a retreat, she asked her boss if she could use a room at GM for meditation. Soon after, she developed an in-house meditation program, which later became the Institute for Mindful Leadership.

She is a hero to corporate meditators everywhere.

9 TO 5

It's true, not all companies are like Google, which has a chief happiness officer and an in-house meditation program, but you might be surprised at how many are following in their footsteps, including General Mills, Aetna, Target, Goldman Sachs, even the US military. Tell that to your boss. While you're at it, show her the stats of increased productivity and decreased sick leave that occur at companies where meditation is included in the wellness program.

SITTING ON THE JOB

Since implementing a mindfulness and gentle yoga program in 2011, the health-care giant Aetna has saved almost $2,000 per employee in health-care costs, and gained close to $3,000 per employee in productivity.

WALKING MEDITATION

LEFT, RIGHT, LEFT

Take a stroll. Hopefully you can go outside and get some nature into your day; otherwise find a secluded hallway at the office.

Set your phone timer for as many minutes as you want.

Now walk. Slowly.

In this meditation, let your anchor be your feet.

Feel the sensation of your feet hitting the ground.

When your mind drifts, get back to the feeling of your feet touching the ground.

When you come to the end of your path, turn around and do it again.

Left, right, left . . .

PROPS AND GEAR

The last thing any of us needs is more stuff. But if more stuff is what gets you to show up every day, then maybe it's worth considering. We are not giving out any points for austerity. Discomfort and pain don't make you a better meditator. We think that whatever makes you show up and want to come back tomorrow is worth looking into.

PiLLOW TALK

If you haven't been able to sit cross-legged since kindergarten, take the pressure off: You don't have to sit on the floor, just sit comfortably. Chairs, sofas, and pillows can help with whatever ails you. Anything works as long as it's not so comfortable that you drift off and fall asleep. There is no need to sit like a swami. Once you become a master meditator or a monk, then you can experiment with sitting on pointy icebergs in Antarctica.

Like all props, cushions are optional, but they are also really helpful. So if you are going to use one, you may as well get one that supports proper alignment so that you have fewer physical distractions during meditation, like excruciating knee pain or hips so tight they may snap in half, or feeling like you are getting stabbed by a machete in the lower back. You will also want to avoid the too-comfy cushion even if it sounds like something you'd enjoy. That's called a beanbag; save it for movie night.

HOW DO YOU KNOW THAT YOU'VE FOUND YOUR CUSHION?

THE GOLDILOCKS TEST:

TOO LOW: You will slump, your knees will kill, your back will hurt, and your head will nod, and it will probably put you to sleep (unless the pain keeps you awake).

TOO HIGH: Your back will curve and pinch, your ankles will cause you agony, your hips will ache, and you will cry.

JUST RIGHT: Your knees will be balanced right below your hips, your back will feel tall and supported, and your soul will shine.

BUCKWHEAT ZAFUS It's for the people who love a pillow-top mattress. It's cushy and conforms to your butt like a pair of cozy sweat pants.

Good for: shorter people and yogis with open hips.

KAPOK ZAFUS If you like a hard mattress and sheets that you can bounce a quarter off of, then this is your cushion. And you probably need it, too.

Good for: tall people and stiff-hipped runners.

ZABUTONS This is for the princess and the pea style of sitting, cushion under cushion. It's for people who need memory foam for their knees and ankles.

Good for: the Tin Man and people with a lot of creaks and cracks.

BACK JACKS Baby steps toward the lotus position all start with the back jack. It's the La-Z Boy of meditation seats.

Good for: everyone, especially if sitting on the floor scares you.

BOLSTERS Bolsters make everything better: they support your back, they give you a physical lift, and they can protect the knees. Use them with any cushion or on their own.

Good for: anyone looking for a little extra support.

BENCHES We don't really know anyone who uses them, but if you are a lapsed Catholic and are missing the pew, we think that you'll love a bench.

Good for: people who love kneeling.

MOOD ENHANCERS

Is there anything I can do that would help get me in the mood to meditate?

Yes, there are all sorts of warm-up tools and activities that will inspire you to sit and get you into meditation mode.

CRYSTALS: Nowadays you don't need to go to a head shop for good hippie gear. You can get it everywhere, from Amazon to 7-Eleven. Crystals are grounding, especially if you hold on to yours while you're meditating. You can also keep it in your change purse or makeup bag for extra-good juju.

TAROT CARDS: A nice way to start a meditation is to pick a card (Tarot, wisdom, energy, chakra, Native medicine, your choice), read the explanation in the book that accompanies the set, and contemplate the message. You might be surprised by the card's psychic powers and its ability to know what's really going on. It's pretty spooky.

ESSENTIAL OILS: Breathe deeply and activate your parasympathetic nervous system. Now do it again, but this time put a few drops of essential oil (lavender, frankincense, or any essence that's peaceful and calming) in your hands, rub them together, and inhale as you start your meditation. Or you can light a candle, then blow it out after a minute or two, and once the wax has created a little puddle, add essential oils to the wax and relight the candle—voilà—a homemade diffuser.

FLOWER ESSENCES: Drink your flowers. The same way that looking at or smelling the roses makes us humans happier, drinking them works even better. It raises your vibrations, lifts your mood, and gives you good energy. There are types for every malady, from fear of roller coasters to the Monday blues. For meditation purposes, start your sit with a few drops.

SOMETHING TO TRY

If you're meditating in the car or somewhere away from your regular space, breathing essential oils can help get you in the meditation mind-set, making it easier to sit.

INCENSE, PALO SANTO, AND SAGE: There is an age-old tradition of using fire in rituals. It clears the heavy energy from the room and adds an element of sacredness, mystery, and beauty. And it smells pretty good, too.

GONGS, BELLS, AND BOWLS: At the start of your session, the sound of the gong or chime is a gentle way to bring your attention inward.

CANDLES: Lighting a candle is a way to start your time on the cushion, and it can also serve as a point of focus for those who meditate with their eyes open.

MUSIC: Music provides an anchor for when following the breath feels a little too elusive. But listen to something soothing and calm, not your spinning playlist.

TIMERS: There are plenty of timers out there. You can spend a lot of money on something fancy or use the timer on your phone. Or don't use a timer. Meditation has been around a lot longer than iPhones. Just sit.

LUCKY CHARMS: Any talisman, special stone, piece of jewelry, coin, fortune cookie reading, or tiny plastic dinosaur will do. Again, this is DIY; it's your practice, it's your magic. Hold it in your hand or place it on your altar.

NOTES FROM THE CUSHION

Dimming the lights can change your state of mind and get you in the meditation mood. Don't make them too low or you might fall asleep.

MEDITATION EXTRAS

SECURITY BLANKET

If you are one of those people who gets chilly when you meditate, then feel free to grab a blanket. Not only will it keep you warm, safe, and cozy, but it also works as a prop to support your knees, ankles, or hands.

TUNE IN

Listening to music can be helpful. Try this: Listen to 3 minutes of music and then turn it off and do 3 minutes of silence. Gradually build up to longer moments without sound.

ALTARED STATES

Meditation altars may seem like they are for serious gurus only, but we are here to tell you that they are for everyone. So if the idea of one intimidates you, we say, try it anyway. Altars don't discriminate; anyone is allowed to have one. They make a space feel safe and sacred and will help you make your meditation practice your own. So do it.

DiY MEDiTATiON ALTAR

PiCK A SPOT: It can be inside or outside, on your bedside table, hidden way in the back of your closet, in the creepy toolshed out back, or out on the fire escape. Put it somewhere that you can get to once or twice a day. When choosing this spot think about sunsets, sunrises, views, people traffic, and noise, and if it's outdoors, consider visitors like pigeons on the fire escape, and mice in the shed. Plan accordingly.

CHOOSE THE ALTAR: It can be something that you already own: a small table, a bookshelf, the top of a dresser, inside a sealed or unused fireplace, a prayer table, a Ms. Pac-Man machine game top, your dashboard, or whatever you want. Again, there are no rules.

CHOOSE YOUR ALTAR OBJECTS: Only choose things that you love, things that bring you joy, happiness, and good energy. Although there are some meditators who choose things that challenge them, like photos of mean people, mementos from childhood bullies, or their exes' old love letters. We think this is very advanced.

SOME IDEAS FOR ALTAR OBJECTS

Mementos: Anything meaningful, personal, or filled with good memories or good luck.

Photos: Images of anything that you love or are inspired by or of whatever is challenging you at the moment.

Malas, rosaries, and Mardi Gras beads.

Candles, Christmas lights, and lanterns: Whatever makes you glow.

Nature: Leaves, plants, dried flowers, small trees, holy water, water from the stream in your backyard, a pet rock, a Chia Pet, or any nature item that you love.

Statues of Ganesh, gurus, and other gods or idols.

Power animal tchotchkes, like elephants and dragonflies.

Mirror: To remind yourself that this is all a reflection of you, and to keep it real.

REMEMBER: Your altar is a sacred space, but sacred doesn't mean serious, so don't be afraid to add a couple of Smurfs or a Holly Hobbie night-light or a ticket stub to the movie that changed your life. Be creative, be you—you can't do this wrong. And no one is watching, anyway.

There is some altar protocol that makes sense to us: First, keep it clean. Since your altar is related to your inner reflection, keep the dust and dirt away. You don't want a dingy soul, do you? And, second, control the clutter; this is an altar, not a junk drawer.

AND FEEL FREE TO CHANGE IT UP WHENEVER YOUR HEART DESIRES.

NOTES FROM THE CUSHION

SLIPPERY SLOPE: Don't be the guy who buys all the latest in running clothing, gear, shoes, and apps and never leaves the couch. Go ahead and get the gear, but don't forget to meditate.

OPEN YOUR EYES

Now that you own a ridiculous amount of meditation gear, why not put some of it to use and try an open-eyed meditation?

1. SIT CROSS-LEGGED or however you like to sit on your new cushion.

2. KEEP YOUR EYES OPEN and focus on an object, perhaps something from your altar.

3. USE SAID OBJECT AS YOUR ANCHOR.

4. WHEN YOUR EYES START TO WANDER (along with your mind) bring it all back to the object or whatever you're focusing on.

5. IF IT BECOMES TOO INTENSE, close your eyes for a few breaths and start again. And again.

NO NEED TO GO iT ALONE: TEACHERS, CLASSES, AND RETREATS

You don't have to go to India to find a guru to learn to meditate. No matter where you live (unless it really is off the grid), there are probably teachers, classes, workshops, and retreats nearby. The key is to find what works for you. Some people need a whole team of enlightened beings while others would prefer to wing it solo. Just see what works for you.

HELP AND SUPPORT

LOOK ONLINE: There is a ton of free stuff on the Internet, from apps to guided sessions, to 21-day challenges, and a million videos. Just start Googling phrases like "guided meditation," "dharma talk," "meditation for morons," "save me," "I think I have a drinking problem," "I want out," and "mediation for a brand new life."

FIND A BUDDY: Having a meditation buddy makes it all the better: someone to meditate with, to go on retreat with, to charge your crystals with, to sing karaoke with, to do ayahuasca with, to move to Mongolia and live in a yurt with, or just someone to talk to about all of this. If none of your friends or family is into it, look online, ask on Facebook, see who's at your yoga class, or join a meditation group.

TEACHERS/CENTERS: Explore and get to know your meditation community. Try different teachers. You may end up at a few different spots before you find someone you connect with.

RETREATS: Retreats are a great way to immerse yourself in the world of meditation. There are probably some in your town or city this weekend. Or if you're looking for an escape, check out the whole wide world.

TEACHER'S PET

THE PSYCHEDELIC PIONEER: RAM DASS

Ram Dass, a former Harvard psychologist, went to India in 1967 and met his guru, Neem Karoli Baba, aka Maharajii, and was forever changed. Dass wrote *Be Here Now*, which changed the world forever. He continues to teach, inspire, and love from his home on Maui.

ON FINDING A TEACHER

If several teachers are available in your area, how do you select one? I say in your area, because you needn't go far afield to begin meditation. To travel all over looking for the perfect teacher adds more to your melodrama than to your liberation. Virtually any teacher is suitable simply to begin, and if no teacher is available, you can do much on your own. In the end, you are your own best teacher.

MEDITATION TRADITIONS TO EXPLORE

VEDIC: A mantra-based form of meditation that is practiced for 20 minutes twice a day. Try it if you need some good vibrations.

ZEN: A sober style of meditation, Zen is bare bones and strict. Posture is important and so are the rules.

VIPASSANA: The opposite of Zen. The rules are lax and the teaching is always free. It focuses on clarity in the mind and opening of the heart—and who doesn't need that?

I AM MEDITATION: Founded by Ramana Maharshi, it's the original DIY meditation. There is no dogma behind it, just you getting to know you through your breath.

TAOIST: It teaches us to focus on any disharmony in the body. It's good for people who are into martial arts or tai chi, or who want more connection to their bodies.

A QUICK STUDY

Don't get caught up in that "I can't start to meditate until I take a class" nonsense. You can start meditating right this second.

Just sit.

You have options. You can learn to meditate on your own, at home, with no formal instruction, by simply watching your own breath, or if you prefer, you can take a class or find a teacher on YouTube or elsewhere online to get started. It's up to you.

GET AWAY

If you have the time, resources, and desire, then we say you should go on a retreat. Try it. But do a little research first.

The benefits of workshops, classes, and retreats in general are:

- Everyone is there for the same reason and the time and the space are dedicated to meditation.
- You won't have to change your daily routine because your daily routine won't exist.
- You'll also be with other people in the same boat—you might even make some new friends.
- And, if you go solo, it's a great place to reinvent yourself (kind of like Los Angeles).

DO YOUR RESEARCH

LEVELS OF LUXURY: Retreats range from the highest of high-end accommodations to donation-only ones: bare bones, sleep on a cot outside, and bring nothing except toothpaste, a toothbrush, and a change of underwear.

KNOW YOUR LIMITS: At some retreats, you will be able to socialize, make friends, talk about what you're learning, even have a glass of wine. At others, you won't have access to a phone or a computer or be allowed to read, eat much, or even speak.

KNOW YOURSELF: Are you in midcrisis? Or are you better than ever? Or are you out of balance? Let these factors help you decide where and when to go on retreat.

THE SKINNY ON RETREATS

A MEDITATION WORKSHOP OR DHARMA TALK

These usually consist of 2 sessions and last anywhere from 1 to 3 hours. Typically, they include a talk, a group meditation, and a Q-and-A session at the end. You might want to try one of these before you commit to going on a retreat.

Remember to wear something comfortable or bring a blanket as you will be doing a lot of sitting. Most likely you will be taking your shoes off, too, so wear clean socks. Bring water and maybe a snack. If you don't like sitting on the floor, there are usually other options: chairs, beanbags, and sit-upons. Turn off your phone, or even better, leave it at home.

STRAIGHT-UP MEDITATION RETREAT

A wonderful way to jump-start your practice and meet other people, some who are new to the whole sitting thing and others who are borderline gurus. We know what you're thinking, but all-day meditation retreats can actually be a lot of fun, as long as you are fun. We recommend bringing a sense of humor, making some friends, and really making the most of meal times. At least that's what we do. Listen, you paid to be there and are there, so show up to all the sessions, ask questions, give in, and be in it. Like everything in life, the more you put in, the more you get out, but with these things, it's even more so.

MiXED-BAG RETREATS

Meditation and yoga, meditation and hiking, meditation and running or chanting or surfing or cooking. There are meditation retreats that are combined with adventure, exercise, even chocolate and wine. There's something for everyone in the hybrid retreat world. They are everywhere: mountains, beaches, jungles, villages in Italy, or on sacred ground in Peru. The upside of the mixed-bag retreat is that you will probably have an easier time convincing your nonmeditating spouse or friend to join you. It is also great to vacation with a purpose. Plus, even if you don't surf, hike, do yoga, or unicycle, it is a perfect place to pick up a new skill. The days usually consist of talks, meditations, and Q-and-As, mixed with the activity of choice. A bit like summer camp for grown-ups.

A SiLENT RETREAT

A day at a silent retreat usually involves sitting in meditation, walking in meditation, eating in meditation, dharma talks, interviews with teachers, siestas, and more meditation. And total silence (except for occasional talks with your teacher). No reading, no texting, no computers, no phones, and not much eating. And, of course, no drinking, no smoking, and no caffeine. It might sound like prison, but most 10-day silent retreats have substantial waiting lists for a reason. They are known to be some of the most life-changing experiences on the planet.

RETREAT RESEARCH CHECKLIST
QUESTIONS TO ASK BEFORE YOU SIGN UP:

Who goes to this thing? If everyone else is a Zen Buddhist and you've never even meditated, you might want to start off elsewhere.

Are cell phones and other electronics allowed?

What practitioners are available? Massage therapists? Energy workers? Astrologers? Psychics? Shamans?

Are there shared rooms or are singles available? Or is it a dormitory situation?

What's the food and drink? Some retreats are vegan, some macrobiotic, and some have more options. Typically the food at retreats is there to fuel you and support your practice. Most retreats offer meals that are easy to digest (meaning no sugar, meats, coffee, booze).

Is there a spa or a place for bodywork? Is there a walking labyrinth? Is there a sweat lodge?

Is there AC? Fans? Open-air camping?

What do the days look like? Is there free time? Should I bring books? Is there Wi-Fi? Can I exercise?

What is the sleeping situation? Big, cozy beds? Cots? Tents? Yurts? Lean-tos?

What's the bathroom situation? Private? Shared? Dorm style? Outdoor? Hole in the ground?

Do they offer medicinals? DMT? Peyote? Ayahuasca? San Pedro?

SOME QUESTIONS YOU MIGHT ASK

Is it a cheat if I sneak coffee into a meditation retreat?

No, but check first because many retreats have coffee or at least caffeinated tea. If your retreat of choice doesn't and you can't live without it, pack some instant. Those instant packs from Starbucks are actually really good.

Can I bring my own food? How about snacks?

Ask before you do. We suggest, for your own sake, that you keep the snacks healthy—nuts, dried fruit, healthy snack bars. Sugar and processed foods have a way of making meditators feel like crap.

What about smoking? I'm trying to quit, but I'm scared to show up without any.

Most retreats will not allow smoking. Again, check first—there may be a smoking area, but we doubt it. We suggest the patch or gum.

I suffer from depression; should I tell the retreat people before I go?

Yes, most retreats will have a form that you fill out that includes mental health questions. Also, if you have a therapist, it's always a good idea to consult with him or her before you go.

Is it better to go solo or with a spouse or friend?

If it's new to you, sometimes it's nice to have a buddy so that you will feel more comfortable and also to have someone to share the experience with. If you go alone, you'll have an entirely different experience; you'll meet people who you probably wouldn't have met and parts of you might come out that otherwise wouldn't have. Who knows, you might be an incredible Sufi dancer, but if you're there with your spouse you may keep that character under wraps. There are pros and cons to each situation and you'll benefit greatly either way.

What should I wear to an all-day meditation workshop?

You can meditate in a towel or a three-piece suit. It's all the same, so whatever makes you feel like showing up is what you should wear.

Do I have to chant?

It depends on the type of retreat, but even if it is one that involves chanting, you don't have to. We say try it. Chanting is like singing. It makes you feel good even if you suck at it.

If I start, do I have to finish?

No. It's not jail. You can leave whenever you want.

I'm worried about the food situation. I'm a meat and potato person, so am I going to starve and be miserable?

We hope not. You won't be burning many calories on a retreat, so you will not be nearly as hungry as normal. But, just in case, bring some snacks with you.

Can I bring sleeping pills to a meditation retreat?

You probably can, but if you're knocked out at night, you might miss out on a lot of good stuff—dreams, insights, and clear, hangover-free mornings. (When dealing with medications, it's always a good idea to check in with your doctor.)

What if I want to skip a day of the retreat?

Then skip it. It's not encouraged, but no one is forcing you to be there. But you should let someone know that you will be MIA that day because they will look for you if you don't show up.

I really want to do a silent retreat, but I can't part ways with my phone when I have 3 kids under 6.

The retreat people have a telephone. It might not be attached to your hip, but people can get in touch with you if there's an emergency. No, you won't be able to call and say good night to your kids, but maybe this will toughen them up a little bit.

TiPS FOR A BETTER RETREAT EXPERIENCE

- **Go with the flow:** Give in to the schedule, the food, and the people as quickly as you can.

- **Try to keep yourself from checking in with the outside world too much:** Be where you are.

- **Enjoy:** Meditation is about lightening up, not making life heavier. Retreats can be fun and funny. Find the laughter.

- **Say yes constantly.**

- **Make friends:** Sit next to someone you don't know. You never know who will teach you something, become your new BFF, help you through the tough days at the retreat, or share a secret chocolate stash with you.

RETREAT PACKING LIST

- [ ] **Cozy clothing:** sweats, yoga pants, T-shirts (keep it simple, create a comfy uniform)

- [ ] **Think in layers:** rooms can be freezing when it's hot out and vice versa. So bring sweaters, scarves, wraps, T-shirts, fleeces, and hoodies.

- [ ] **Remember it's a retreat,** not a fashion show. It's also not a great place to wear racy clothing.

- [ ] **Running shoes** or something similar to explore in.

- [ ] **Water bottle**

- [ ] **Earplugs:** they are great if you have a roommate who snores.

- [ ] **Journal and pen**

- [ ] **Drugs:** painkillers, aspirin, Dramamine, Neosporin, Tums, hydrocortisone.

- [ ] **Light snacks:** nuts, bars, vitamin C packs.

- [ ] **Small tote bag:** to carry things around the retreat with you.

- [ ] **Light blanket:** if you get cold easily.

- [ ] **Lightweight raincoat**

- [ ] **Insect repellent**

- [ ] **Small flashlight**

- [ ] **Sunscreen/sunglasses/sun hat**

- [ ] **Hand wipes**

- [ ] **Personal products:** bring unscented stuff.

- [ ] A small-sized **laundry soap:** to wash things in your sink.

- [ ] **Books**

- [ ] **Cash**

- [ ] **Something from home:** photos of your kids or a talisman or lucky charm.

Make yourself a little card to carry in your wallet with your emergency contact information and medical information (it's good to have whenever you travel solo).

IF YOU FIND A GREAT RETREAT, GREAT.

IF YOU FIND A GREAT TEACHER, GREAT.

BUT YOU CAN LEARN AS MUCH OR MUCH MORE FROM A TREE OR A RIVER AS LONG AS YOU ARE QUIET ENOUGH.

DIY RETREAT

Short on funds? Time? But still want to go on a retreat? Then create your own.

The more you plan it out in advance, the more successful it will be. Trust us, if you try to wing a DIY meditation retreat, it'll be way too easy to opt out and waste the days off watching bad TV or reorganizing the garage.

1 Decide how many days you want to do this for. Then free up your schedule as if you were going away for real.

2 Are you doing this solo or with a friend or a group? Plan accordingly.

3 Decide what kind of a retreat you would like to do: all meditation, meditation and exercise, yoga, silent, moments or times of silence, a dance party, a retreat with wine-and-cheese breaks, or the opposite, a 3-day fast.

4 Is it going to be in your home or somewhere outside: a cabin, a tent, a beach, your basement, or your sister's backyard?

5 Decide on food. Will you be vegetarian? Vegan? Starving? Where is the food coming from? Do you need to prepare it before the retreat? Or order it in advance? Do you need to do a big grocery trip?

6 Set an intention for the retreat: What do you hope to get from it? What's the purpose? Don't be vague.

7 Decide how much interaction you will have with the outside world: Will you have designated times for cell phone, computer, electronics? Or turn them off all together? If all together, then let people know. Do an automated response with your email; call your mom and tell her.

8 Then, after all the big decisions are made, plan out the days:

- Decide on a wake-up time.
- Decide on meditation times: How many sessions per day (we suggest morning, afternoon, and evening)?
- Are you going to use online talks: dharma talks, guided meditations, podcasts?
- If you are including yoga, are you going to classes or doing it on your own or online?
- If there will be exercise, are you going to a class or doing it on your own?
- Will there be creative time? Journal writing, painting, sketching, playing the piano, singing, square dancing, collage making, knitting, pottery, or whatever you like?
- Will there be reading time?
- Will there be siesta time?
- Will there be self-care or spa time? It can be anything from a bubble bath to a swim in the ocean. We really like Chinese foot massages.

POSTRETREAT TIPS:
REENTRY TO THE REAL WORLD

Some people return from a retreat and go straight back into their regular lives without flinching, while others have a hard time transitioning from retreat mode into mommy mode or work mode or crappy marriage mode. Real life can sometimes feel abrupt, like the volume is too high, the world is too busy, and life is just too much. So for those of you who have a tough time with reentry, we have some helpful tips that will make coming back a little smoother and will help you retain that postretreat glow.

- Meditate: Keep it going, that's the whole point.

- Plan: If you're traveling to and from your retreat, try to schedule it so that you arrive early enough to get a good night's sleep or, even better, have the next day off. Depending on what you were eating, slowly transition back (or keep it going), but be nice to your stomach.

- Lay off the booze. Don't go on a bender as soon as you step off the plane.

- Get lots of sleep.

- Be considerate: Don't be the guy who tries to change everyone around you because you went on a meditation retreat.

- Don't forget to keep the good juju going as long as possible.

CHAPTER 5

THE BODY ELECTRIC

HOW TO SIT

There are people (not you, of course) who don't or can't or won't meditate because it's too uncomfortable, but that is because of that age-old legend that says you have to sit in a certain way to meditate properly. We are here to tell you that this is not true. But we are also here to tell you that how you sit helps immensely. Life is a paradox. Didn't you know that?

Posture is powerful. You don't have to be in agony, but a little discomfort goes a long way in terms of alertness, energy, and connection. A lot of magic happens when you plug in and plug in correctly. As much as we hate a rule, sitting with intention will connect you to the secrets of the universe, whereas slumping on the couch may cause dullness and apathy.

Are your shoulders slumping? Are they at your ears? Is your jaw tense? Are you clenching your fists? Are you tapping your foot? Twirling your hair? Biting your lip? How aware are you of what you are doing with your body?

If you can't connect to your body, how are you going to connect to your emotions? Your thoughts? Your heart? Your soul? Connecting to the body isn't hard, but it's something you have to do consciously or you and your body will drift apart. Or, God forbid, consciously uncouple. And who wants that?

BODY-SCAN MEDITATION

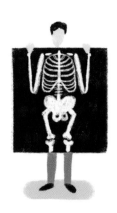

Why not connect with your lovely body?
Try this when you are feeling unmoored:

1 Take a seat or, if possible, lie down.

2 Close your eyes.

3 Rest your hands on your stomach.

4 Take a couple of deep belly breaths to ground yourself.

5 Breathe in, through your feet all the way up to the top of your head.

6 Exhale back through your body down to your feet.

7 What does the left leg feel like? The right? Are they heavy? Light? Tense? Relaxed? Restless? Take notice.

8 Move on to your ankles, your feet, each of your toes.

9 Imagine a submarine exploring inside of you and watch as it tours around your whole body.

10 Allow the submarine to travel through your stomach, arms, fingers, hands, funny bones, shoulders, elbows, neck, back, head, face, and nose.

11 When you find yourself daydreaming about your next meal, gently bring yourself back to your body and breath.

12 Do this for 7 minutes or 7 hours.

13 Feel every nook and cranny of your body. Feel the tense spots, the stored emotions, the old aches and pains, the new black-and-blues, the forgotten memories, the undiscovered treasures, and the genuine joy that comes from connection.

POSTURES FOR ALL OF MY FRIENDS

NONE of these are ways that you have to sit—they are merely suggestions that have worked for people for the past 5,000 years.

BENDY BETTY

FULL LOTUS: A good posture for Betty and her pals, but for most of us it's a pipe dream because our tight hips won't, even let us consider it. But for those of you who can do it, its the über pose and has been for thousands of years. If you can get yourself there, do it; you'll feel energized, alive, and open to the world.

HALF BETTY

HALF LOTUS: Easier than a full lotus, but it still might be tough for peeps with tight hips or creaky knees. Definitely give it a try, and if your foot can't make it to your thigh, try the calf (quarter lotus). Over time it'll get easier to reach the thigh.

PRE-K BETTY

CROSS-LEGGED: An oldie but a goodie. Most of us learned this one in kindergarten and some of us haven't sat this way since, but it's a great posture for those who can't quite contort themselves into a lotus or a half lotus but are still comfortable sitting on the ground with crossed legs.

STRAIGHT-UP BETTY

BURMESE POSITION: If you feel like you are slouching while sitting cross-legged, try the Burmese position: legs in front but with calves and feet on the floor or cushion.

SISTER BETTY

KNEELING: If you're into kneeling, try a bench or you can use a pillow or yoga bolster.

SEATED BETTY

SITTING IN A CHAIR: For some people, the floor is a no-go zone, but not to worry because that's why chairs were invented. To meditate in a chair (properly), your feet need to be touching the ground, if they don't reach, prop them with a book or a box. Sit away from the back of the chair so that you aren't resting against it.

DON'T LET IT GO TO YOUR HEAD, BETTY

UPSIDE DOWN: There are lots of ways to get upside down: headstand, handstand, yoga swing, hammock, on the couch, antigravity boots, hang from a pull-up bar or a tree—really any way you can get there is great even if it's only for 30 seconds. Being upside down is antiaging, changes your perspective, improves mood, decreases back pain, improves brain function, decreases anxiety and stress, makes you laugh, decreases varicose veins, and increases focus.

90-DEGREE-ANGLE BETTY

LEGS ON THE WALL: Lie on the floor with your legs up against the wall. Great for easing stress, reducing lower back pain, lessening anxiety, calming the nerves, and reducing swelling.

STEADY BETTY

STANDING: Tadasana. Good for crowded train rides, long lines, and anywhere you are stuck on your feet.

REBEL BETTY

NO-POSTURE: Twirl like a Sufi dancer, stomp like a shaman, sway with the music, or just plain move. Good for lifting the spirits, increasing joy, and finding your groove.

SiT LiKE A SWAMi: HiNTS FOR A BETTER SiT

- Be where your body is. You can get as much out of meditation in a chair as you can in any pose, as long as you are focused and present.

- You can sit on the couch, but try not to sit like a sack of potatoes. If you go into it like a slob, what do you think you'll get out of it?

- We don't recommend lying down (unless you have a medical condition that requires it). Often, lying down makes it too easy to get tired or fall asleep. But, hey, if it works for you, then go ahead.

- It helps to pretend that there is a string coming out of the top of your head. Let it pull you up like a puppet coming to life. Once your head is up, keep it there with the support of the imaginary string.

FACE TIME

PRIVATE EYES

Keeping your eyes shut can help you feel safe and contained while sitting. But if you want to work on your focus, keep them open; that's what candles and cute effigies are for. The choice is yours.

BREATHING LESSON

Breathe with your nose unless you physically can't. The nose filters the air, gets it to the right temperature, calms you down, and makes it easier for you to meditate.

LOCKJAW

If your jaw feels tense while you meditate, bring your focus to your jaw and feel and observe the tension. Breathe into it and let it go. Repeat over and over for the rest of your life.

TONGUE-TIED

Relax your tongue and let it float to the roof of your mouth and gently close your lips.

GIVE ME A HAND

Hands can rest gently on the thighs with palms up or down. If you want to create more of an intention with your hands, then opt for a mudra. Mudras (positions) are a form of prayer, a way of carrying your intent in your meditation. Traditionally the hands were given mudras to create a certain energy, which is far more effective then letting them flop around like a couple of fish.

SOME MUDRAS YOU MIGHT LIKE

DHYANA MUDRA

The left hand lies in the right and the thumbs kiss.

Good for: fragile mental states, hangovers, sad sots, or people on the verge.

APAN MUDRA

Place the thumb, middle finger, and ring finger together and extend the index finger and pinkie.

Good for: those in need of a detox, a metabolism boost, a soul cleansing, or just a good cry.

JNANA MUDRA

Place the tip of the thumb on the index finger in the "okay" position. Then point the other three fingers toward the sky.

Good for: good energy, good juju, good vibrations, and a good life.

PRAN MUDRA

Place the thumb, ring finger, and pinkie together and extend the index and middle fingers.

Good for: alertness, assertiveness, confidence, and vitality. It's like liquid courage without the hangover.

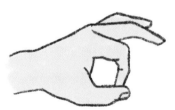

CHIN MUDRA

Place the tip of the thumb on the index finger in the "okay" position. Let the other three fingers point down.

Good for: amnesiacs and people with foggy brains (pregnant women, heavy drinkers, and potheads).

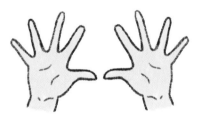

JAZZ HANDS

Place both hands by the face with palms spread and facing out.

Good for: laughter and forgetting.

A HANDY MEDITATION, AKA MEDITATE WITH A MUDRA

1 CHOOSE A MUDRA.

2 CLOSE YOUR EYES.

3 FOCUS ON YOUR BREATH.

4 NOTICE THAT WHEN YOUR MIND WANDERS, YOUR HAND WILL DROP THE MUDRA.

5 WHEN YOUR HAND RELEASES, COME BACK TO THE BREATH AND THE MUDRA.

STAYING ALIVE

If you are new to sitting and it hurts—your knees hurt, your back hurts, your shoulders hurt—and all you can do is focus on the pain, do not fret. This is normal. As long as you don't have a broken neck or something, you're probably fine. You are not alone; many people experience discomfort while meditating. Notice the pain and watch what your mind does. Is it trying to end the session? Don't let it run away from you.

QUICK FIXES FOR DISCOMFORT

- Are your hips above your knees? If not, lower the knees.
- Is your spine straight? If not, sit up.
- Is your core engaged? If not, take a deep belly breath.
- Are you a ball of tension? If so, relax.

MEDITATION ACHES AND PAINS

There are many ways to sit in meditation, and postures for every ailment, complication, and level of discomfort. There are ways to sit that you never even imagined and might not even want to, but we will show you anyway.

 STIFF KNEES: Sit cross-legged on your cushion with a yoga block or cushion under each knee.

 ACHY BACK: Place your cushion against the wall with a bolster perpendicular to the cushion so that your back is supported against the bolster. Add yoga blocks or cushions under your knees for more support.

 SORE SHOULDERS: Rest your hands on a rolled-up blanket on your lap. It will release the pressure from your shoulders.

 POINTY ANKLES: Roll a blanket lengthwise and place it underneath your ankles and feet when you sit cross-legged.

 TIGHT HIPS: If possible, sit in the Burmese position and place sandbags on each thigh (the yoga type of sandbags). They will help to stabilize your seat, open up your hips, and prepare you for the big day when you can do lotus.

 SLEEPY FEET: Keep your feet flexed if they have a tendency to snooze.

STiFF AS A BOARD

Sitting in meditation can take a toll on a body that isn't used to it. Try stretching before you sit. That's why yoga was invented.

STRET(HES FOR SiTTERS

EMPTY THE MiND: Before you sit, stand and hang over your body. Release the stress for a few minutes and feel all the crazy thoughts fall out of the top of your head. A second option is to hold on to the back of a chair as you hang.

OPEN UP AND SAY OHM: To open the hips and stretch the glutes, hold on to that same chair and cross your ankle over your knee (create a 4) and then pull away, while sitting down in an air chair.

LEAN iN: Sit on the ground with your legs straight out in front of you. Bend and gently reach for your toes or calves or knees.

STRET(H AND SHiNE: Touch the bottoms of your feet together and bend the knees so that your legs are in a diamond in front of you. Either bring the feet superclose to the body or keep them in the diamond. Then bend forward and stay there for a few minutes, taking deep breaths into your hips and lower back.

GENTLE PRETZEL: Sit in an easy pose and twist to the right, then place your right hand on the floor behind your back. Keep your left hand on your right knee. Stay for a few breaths, then with each breath twist more deeply and then switch to the other side.

FIDGETY

Can't sit still? Do you go to the movies? Watch TV? Go to your kids' sport games? Go to church? Or temple? Or do you mean you can't sit still without being entertained? Give yourself a chance. In the beginning it's difficult to sit and do nothing, but focus on the breath or the mantra. It's new, awkward, and can feel a little anticlimactic. Learning to sit with awkwardness, discomfort, and a lack of outside entertainment is the practice, and that's where the magic begins.

CHEATS TO HELP YOU SIT STILL

- Use a heating pad or an electric blanket for added comfort.
- Sit with a friend or spouse or partner.
- Hold your cat or dog or chinchilla or baby on your lap.
- Meditate in the tub or sauna or Jacuzzi.
- Put a beauty mask on and sit for 15 minutes.

NOTES FROM THE CUSHION

The best cheat for difficulty with sitting still is adding movement. Sukey loves tai chi because of the inner stillness that she is able to tap into. But all that stillness comes from movement. Qigong is pretty great, too. Just go with the flow.

FREEZE TAG

In some formal meditation practices, sitting perfectly still is highly esteemed. If this interests you, you should explore such practices. Otherwise, a little movement isn't a big deal. But if you are getting up and off your cushion, changing your seat constantly, switching the cross of your legs, or scratching every itch, you might have monkey body. If that's the case, we recommend getting up and dancing or shaking it out and then coming back to sit and meditate.

CHANGE YOUR STATE AND MEDITATE

EXERCISE

GO UPSIDE DOWN

DO THE WORM

SUFI DANCE

HULA-HOOP

BELLY DANCE

JUGGLE

PAIN, PAIN, GO AWAY

How do I know if pain is real pain or if it's resistance to meditation?

Real pain sucks; you will know it, we promise. HINT: If you're questioning it, then it's not real pain.

Meditation is a potent technique for managing physical pain, whether it is a headache, heartache, hangover, hay fever, hernia, hemorrhoids, Hashimoto's disease, hemophilia, or hot flashes. In fact, there are studies that show that meditation works better than drugs, even morphine.

PAINKILLER MEDITATION

1 Sit as comfortably as you can.

2 Close your eyes and focus on your hot spots, aka pain areas.

3 Breathe in and fill the hot spots with your breath.

4 Hold that sensation and let it go.

5 Breathe out and release any pain that you can with the breath.

6 Notice how that even in pain, there can be a heightening and a lowering of sensation. But really get on the outside of it as much as possible and watch. Stay with the pain as opposed to describing it to yourself (that won't help).

I feel like meditation is making me more tired and not energizing me.

Meditation is not cocaine. Sometimes you feel energized from it and other times it might feel like Sleepytime tea. But if the exhaustion is really a thing, then perhaps it's a good idea to check in and ask yourself some questions:

- Is the room too hot?
- Am I dehydrated?
- Am I under extra stress?
- Am I feeling anxious? Blue?
- Am I being emotionally drained in everyday life?
- How is my posture? Perhaps lying down isn't such a good idea.
- Is it 3 a.m.?
- Am I jetlagged?
- Is it my meds?
- Am I exercising too much or too hard?
- Or perhaps I just need more sleep?

NO DOZE: WAKE UP BEFORE YOU SIT

LION'S BREATH

Inhale through your nose and exhale strongly through your mouth (make a "HA" sound). As you exhale, open your mouth wide and stick out your tongue, making it point toward the floor. You might want to refrain from doing this at work, on a bus, or in a crowded elevator.

FOOD FOR THOUGHT

Is it better to sit on an empty stomach or after you've eaten?

If you eat a big meal before you meditate, you will probably be very sleepy because your body will be busy with all that digestion. And meditation takes only 20 minutes, so you won't starve to death. Drink a glass of water instead.

GIVE ME FEVER

Should I meditate if I am feeling sick?

Yes, meditate if you feel blue, have a slight fever, or have a low-grade hangover. Just notice whatever ails you with the same kindness you would give a good friend. It is an excellent way to nurse yourself back to health.

IT HAPPENS

I like to meditate at night. Does it work if I have had a couple of drinks?

Try it and see how you feel. Some people are fine with it and others feel like it's a sacrilege. We think if it works for you then it's fine.

THE CHAKRAS: GET YOUR GROOVE BACK

Chakras are spinning wheels of energy located along your spine. There are 7 chakras and each has a specific location, serves a particular purpose, and holds a whole lot of good juju. The thing is, chakras can get easily blocked, which is our body's way of telling us what needs looking at. The body doesn't lie.

CROWN: connection to the universe, who you are beyond your body, spirituality, freedom.

THIRD EYE: intuition, insights, inner wisdom, trust, open-mindedness.

THROAT: truth, self-expression, communication, emotions, ability to listen.

HEART: compassion, forgiveness, unconditional love, acceptance.

SOLAR PLEXUS: fire, power, self-esteem, productivity, confidence, risk-taking.

SACRAL: relationships, sexuality, creativity, sense of abundance, positivity, flow, fertility.

ROOT: feeling of belonging, family ties, survival, safety, and basic needs.

CHAKRA MEDITATION

You can do this meditation in one of two ways, either clean house and do the whole meditation, going over each chakra one by one; or focus on only one chakra, the one that most resonates with you because that is probably the chakra that needs some work.

1. Sit comfortably.

2. Close your eyes.

3. Start at the base of your spine, the root chakra. Imagine the color red. In your mind, repeat the word "LAM." Hold the color and the sound until you feel ready to move to the next chakra.

4. Move your attention to below your navel, the sacral chakra. Imagine the color orange. In your mind, repeat the word "VAM." Hold the color and the sound until you feel ready to move to the next chakra.

5. Move your attention to above the navel, the solar plexus chakra. Imagine the color yellow. In your mind, repeat the word "RAM." Hold the color and the sound until you feel ready to move to the next chakra.

6. Move your attention to your heart, the heart chakra. Imagine the color green. In your mind, repeat the word "YAM." Hold the color and the sound until you feel ready to move to the next chakra.

7. Move your attention to your throat, the throat chakra. Imagine the color turquoise. In your mind, repeat the word "HAM." Hold the color and the sound until you feel ready to move to the next chakra.

8. Move your attention to just between your eyebrows, the third eye chakra. Imagine the color indigo. In your mind, repeat the word "SHAM." Hold the color and the sound until you feel ready to move to the next chakra.

9. Move your attention to the crown of your head, the crown chakra. Imagine the color violet. In your mind, repeat the word "AUM." Hold the color and the sound until

you are ready to work your way back down to the root chakra, by doing this meditation in reverse. The reason for doing this, going through the chakras from the base up and then from the crown down, is because each chakra builds on the other.

UNBLOCK THE CHAKRAS

Each chakra has its own energy and power, so you might choose to focus on something specific depending on what ails you.

ROOT	Neediness, insecurity, woe-is-me vibes.
SACRAL	Frigidity, guilt, self-loathing, and all-around bad energy.
SOLAR PLEXUS	Depression, dullness, fear, and complacency.
HEART	Codependency, dysfunction, addiction, and negativity.
THROAT	Shyness, communication issues, denial, passivity, lying, and lack of connection.
THIRD EYE	Suspicion, jealousy, trust issues, cynicism, and paranoia.
CROWN	Egoism, self-centeredness, arrogance, all-about-me syndrome.

NOTES FROM THE CUSHION

Chakra meditations are big healers. Sukey originally started meditating because of them. When she was just a little fledgling sitter, she was still recovering from the sexual trauma she had experienced as a teenager. She had been a singer, but she stopped because of the unaddressed trauma. Her voice was gone. To get it back, not only did she do a ton of chakra work on the throat, but she had to combine it with the sacral, to complete the healing. After that, her whole life changed.

SPRING CHICKEN

THE WHIRLING DERVISH: TAO PORCHON-LYNCH

Born on August 13, 1918, Tao is a master yoga teacher, author, activist, actress, oenophile, vegetarian, and meditator. She holds the *Guinness Book of World Records* for being the world's oldest yoga teacher. She is almost 100 years old and still teaches 6 to 8 classes a week. Deepak Chopra says that she is an example of *Ageless Body, Timeless Mind.* If that's not enough, she took up ballroom dancing at 85 and is now a competitive dancer with partners as much as 70 years her junior.

Tao's mantra is: **There is nothing you cannot do.**

Your breath doesn't know how old you are. The most vital thing in the world is learning to breathe. People think they know how, but they don't. The practices of yoga and meditation help you live each moment and get in touch with your life force. When you feel this energy within yourself, you feel alive and are able to pass this on to others.

From *The National,*
2/10/16

CHAPTER 6

MIND GAMES: WHO IS RUNNING YOUR SHOW?

So many of us resist meditation because we hate sitting there like a sitting duck. It makes us feel vulnerable, uncomfortable, and stupid. Most of us suck at connecting with ourselves, being still, and feeling what comes up. We are conditioned and trained to quash discomfort as soon as we feel the tiniest pang.

But a large part of this process, this learning to meditate process, is developing a tolerance for sitting with uncomfortable feelings. In order to deal with your shit and have a way better life, you've got to be willing to show up and sit in the muck.

First things first. MEDITATION DOES NOT MEAN YOU STOP THINKING, nor does it mean that you ever get to a point where your head is completely empty. That'd be really cool, but it doesn't happen, at least not to any living person that we know. Thoughts will come and go, and at the beginning they will come and go often, quickly, and, yes obsessively. That's called resistance. You want to sit, but you don't.

WHAT AM i COOKiNG TONiGHT?
WHY DOES HE ALWAYS RUiN EVERYTHING?
DiD i PAY THE PHONE BiLL?
WHY DiD i DO THAT?
MY BOSS HATES ME
i'M LATE AGAiN

PLACES TO SEND THAT PESKY MIND CHATTER

THOUGHT RIVER: When thoughts come in, watch them float away above your head on Thought River.

DOWN THE ROAD: Send them on their way like uninvited guests, but gently. Don't slam the door on them, just say thank you for showing up today but I'm not interested.

THE BUBBLE GRAVEYARD: Imagine if each thought that arises is in a bubble. As the bubbles appear, pop them and watch them disappear.

THOUGHT DETOX MEDITATION

1 Take a seat.

2 Close your eyes.

3 Take 3 deep belly breaths.

4 Notice each inhale and exhale while breathing deeply and slowly.

5 Choose a place to send mind chatter (see above) and consciously notice each thought and send it to your chosen place.

6 Continue for 5 to 15 minutes.

THE MiND: WHAT COMES UP

Meditation will bring your stuff up, and not just your blissful, happy, loving, joyous stuff, but after some time on the cushion, it will be far easier to accept all of it, even the difficult stuff. Accepting everything removes the charges that our feelings carry. Just sit with them. They won't bite you.

Thoughts are just thoughts. Uncomfortable thoughts, weird thoughts, creepy thoughts, bad, mad, sad, evil thoughts enter everyone's mind, so let them. By allowing them to share the stage with all of your other thoughts, they lose their power. They're just thoughts; they don't own you.

WATCH THE BOREDOM

Boredom is just another form of resistance, so pay attention to it. What does it look like? Feel like? Where is it coming from? What are you not allowing yourself to experience? What is the fear?

WATCH THE STEW

If you are in any sort of snit or rage, sit now in the heat of the moment. It will calm you down so that you don't do something stupid or regretful. It will change your state of mind and take the edge off.

Stewing is another word for getting hijacked by your thoughts. Letting go is not buying into it; it's stepping back and watching the thoughts and not falling for them. That is how you stop the stew.

WATCH OUT FOR THE MEDITATION BLUES

Whether you have a good experience or one that you don't love, you're setting yourself up for a disappointment if you try to repeat anything. The only thing you can do with a good session (and a bad one) is to let it go. Comparison never works, nor do expectations. Do it every time like it's the first time and you and will never have a bad session, just a session.

WATCH OUT FOR THE GROCERY LISTS

If you find yourself making to-do lists and getting too much done while you are meditating, pay attention to it. The lists will lose their sense of urgency as you notice them; they'll still come up (all the time), but they won't be so important.

WATCH OUT FOR THE PROGRESS REPORTS

Progress with meditation is not so easy to measure. It's not like you can get on a scale and see how much weight you've dropped. And unless you have an fMRI machine at home, there really isn't any measuring to be done.

Sometimes you'll notice the effects immediately, but as for longer-term, longer-lasting benefits, they usually come out of the blue when you have a realization like, Wow, or I didn't react like I normally do, or When did I get so patient or compassionate or understanding?

We've been duped into believing that the good stuff will create instantaneous change. Pop a pill and become a new person. Sadly, with meditation and anything genuine, it doesn't work that way. Just show up every day. That's your mission. We promise your life will indeed be shifted, altered, changed, and much better. Show up and stop worrying about what you get in return.

WATCH OUT FOR THE MEAN WATCHER

When you sit to meditate, do so with kindness and compassion so that when thoughts arise, you can gently watch them without judgment. When we add negative or aggressive energy, even to the watching of the innocent little thoughts, it layers the practice with negativity and it shuts down our ability to sit back and see ourselves with acceptance and love.

WATCH OUT FOR BRILLIANCE

Aha moments, creative downloads, answers to difficult mathematical equations, solutions to the world's problems, brilliant ideas—all of these things may come up while you are simply sitting in meditation, and we should hope they do. You may wonder what you should do when it happens. Should you stop sitting and grab a pen and paper? Perhaps, if it's that good, we say write it down. But most of the time, pay attention and keep meditating; if it's that life-changing, you won't forget it in the next 11 minutes.

YOU CANNOT EXPERiENCE THE TRUTH iF YOU CONTiNUE TO TELL YOUR STORY AND YOU CANNOT CONTiNUE TO TELL YOUR STORY iF YOU ARE EXPERiENCiNG THE TRUTH.

GANGAJi

We are all mad storytellers, which is great around the campfire, but not so great when it's in your head. The stories that we've made up and believe about ourselves, the stories that have conditioned us since we could talk, the stories that have literally run our lives, these stories are the stories that need to go, but before we can drop them, we need to know what they are, to identify them.

The first clue to locating the story is knowing that it is in the past. There is no such thing as the story if you are living in the present. The story is something that happened (or didn't happen) once upon a time and has stuck ever since. It's formed you, or so you think.

The second clue to finding the story is noticing what it is that gets your goat, has your number, gets under your skin, rubs you the wrong way, and ruffles your feathers. Because, when you start to feel these things, the story is doing its job.

So once we discover where the story lives, how do we dump it and move on with our lives? We have two suggestions, either start meditating or schedule a lobotomy.

SOUND FAMILIAR?

A story, whether true or not, is still a story. It doesn't mean anything unless you assign meaning to it. We forget that all the time. Meditation pulls you outside of the story so that you can see it. If you are confused, here are some examples of stories and the self-prophesizing power that they hold.

STORIES WILL PLAY THEMSELVES OUT FOREVER IF YOU LET THEM.

I am not a commitment person.

My sister is the pretty one.

I'm big-boned.

I have no self-discipline.

I'm Type A.

I'm the golden child.

I'm a pleaser.

I'm too much.

I'm not math smart.

I'm not a runner.

We aren't creative types.

I'm socially awkward.

I'm the man of the house.

I always date jerks.

Better to have someone than be alone.

I'll always be alone.

No one gets me.

I'm the shy one.

I've always been the caretaker.

Bad things always happen to me.

I walk around with a rain cloud over me.

I'm accident prone.

I'm not a public speaker.

I'm a slow learner.

I'm an extrovert.

He's the funny one.

I'm not fun unless I drink.

I am a control freak.

I'm not the motherly type.

I'm not spiritual.

Girls don't do that.

Boys don't cry.

I have a hard time saying no.

I'm not confrontational.

THE DEEP DIG

These stories become our identities, but they are important only because we make them so; we give them meaning and go into a lifetime contract with them. The only way to break that contract is to become aware of the stories in the first place and of how they operate through us. Once you do that, they begin to slip away. But it's not as easy as it sounds.

What stories are stuck on repeat in your brain? They are typically so embedded that it's difficult to see that they are just stories. We make them into mountains that won't budge, and we give them that kind of weight and that kind of sacredness. This stuff is slippery and deeply ingrained into our way of living, so it can be tricky to figure out what's what.

AN ARCHAEOLOGY OF SELF

Take a little time to answer the questions that follow. It's better if you write them out but not in the book. Don't be lazy. Go get a piece of paper and a pen and answer them honestly (you can throw the paper away when you are finished, or burn it, or hang it on the wall). The point of this exercise is to recognize your story and to see what is running your show.

PART 1: GETTING TO KNOW YOU

1. How would you describe your role in your family?

2. How would your mother (or father or siblings) describe you?

3. Who were you in your family?

4. What kind of person are you in your relationship with your partner?

5. What kind of person are you in your relationship with your close friends?

6. What do you reveal about yourself on a first date?

7. What do you reveal about yourself in a job interview?

8. What do you reveal about yourself to a stranger on a plane?

9. What do you reveal about yourself to a new (but soon to be very good) friend?

10. What do you reveal about yourself on social media?

11. What do you reveal about your life, past, and childhood to a new partner once you're intimate?

12. What do you reveal about your life, past, and childhood to a therapist?

13. What do you reveal about your life, past, and childhood to a friend you haven't seen in 20 years?

14. And what don't you reveal to any of the above people?

Chances are, you have a pretty defined narrative (story) with a ton of subplots just like a great English novel. These are all big fat clues as to what your story is. If you're confused, just ask your best friend or sister.

PART 2: THE STORY OF MY LIFE

1. What have you told yourself you couldn't do because of a childhood story?

2. How has that story affected your relationships?

3. How does it manipulate you in relationships?

4. How has it shut you down?

5. How much power/control does it have?

6. How has it made you sick? Or fat? Or skinny? Or addicted? Or anxious? Or depressed?

7. How has your story caused you to self-flagellate? Or self-destruct? Or self-hate? Or to live in a I-am-not-enough syndrome?

8. What benefits did you get from that childhood story? How has the story served you?

9. Has it aided your success or gotten you special treatment (like the person who was ignored by her parents, but then became independent and later a huge success because of it)?

This isn't a personality test. The reason to really think about and answer these questions is to identify what is driving you. Your thoughts, emotions, and behavior all stem from this stuff. Meditation is a tool that helps you to detach from the story to be able to see where and how said story is affecting you. In order to let this stuff go (get rid of the story), it's helpful to understand how it operates in you in the first place. So just sit. You are a lot more than your story.

TRIGGER HAPPY

If you are having a tough time with this whole story thing, think back to your last family get-together. Whether it was for a big holiday or a Sunday dinner, it can be a challenging time, where sane, independent adults fall back into their childhood roles and cause one another a lot of pain, anger, remorse, humiliation, and regret.

The key is to know that if you are human, you will get triggered, especially by the people who raised you, who love you the most. It's difficult to slow down and see what is happening while it's happening. But we have a few extremely helpful tricks for these exact situations:

1. When you feel triggered by your spouse, partner, sibling, parent, or close family member, imagine instead your next-door neighbor or child's teacher saying the exact same thing to you. Does it have the same power? Do you hate him/her? Do you blame him/her? Do you think that person is pure evil and out to get you? That he/she doesn't understand you? Probably not.

2. When you feel your blood beginning to heat up, really notice the physical sensations that the triggers cause. They feel like emotional hot spots. Feel them and breathe into them. Don't speak; instead, just breathe into those little hot spots like your life depends on it.

3. Watch yourself get triggered; watch your physical sensations, your emotional responses, your story playing in your mind; watch the other person; watch the situation; watch it like you are in the front row at a Broadway show. This is the practice. This is where triggers go to die. This is freedom.

4. Love them more. Your family. Your friends. Your community. Your emenies. Everyone and anyone. Love them more.

STUCK ON THE STORY

Some people love their stories, like the guy who grew up with nothing, in extremely hard circumstances, and overcame all sorts of stuff. That's a great story, but it's still a story. It doesn't mean he can't share it and inspire others with it, but to grow he needs to let it go and live in the now.

Look, it's almost impossible to completely drop your story—it seeps in everywhere, all of the time. But observe it. Notice it. Watch it and see how it affects you.

YOU ARE NOT ANGRY
YOU ARE NOT NERVOUS
YOU ARE NOT DEPRESSED
YOU ARE NOT SAD
YOU ARE NOT SCARED

You are merely experiencing these things. We latch on to emotions as if they are permanent. Nothing is permanent. All of the above and the 10,000 other feelings that hit us on a daily basis are fleeting. In order to not turn a bout of the blues into a permanent cloud above our heads, we have to recognize them when they appear, feel them, and then let them go.

If you describe yourself as an angry person, you will spend hours every day feeling pretty upset. It's a self-fulfilling prophecy. It is just a story, an age-old story that has gotten into your bones. You are a guy who has experienced anger. That's it. No need to make it one of your personality traits. In the same way, someone who says, "I am deppresed" would benefit by changing the language (dropping the story) to "I am experiencing depression." Same goes for the sad, the anxious, the fearful, the lonely, and all the rest of us who give a lifelong story to a nagging emotion.

No matter what I do, I can't lose weight. I'm 40 pounds over-weight and can't drop it. Do I need a skinny story?

No, you don't need a skinny story or any story, including the story that got you there in the first place. What might help is:

- **Meditation:** To notice the stories you are telling yourself.

- **Acceptance:** Become accountable and show up for yourself in a really kind way (because no one else will).

- **Awareness:** Watch when the story is entering the scene. Notice when you head for the fridge. What's driving the craving?

- **Self-love:** When you stop being hijacked by the story, you'll start taking better care of yourself, and that's letting it go.

SHED THE STORY

THE FITNESS LEGEND: RICHARD SIMMONS

Richard Simmons weighed 268 pounds when he finished high school. After trying every fad diet and nearly starving himself to death, he dropped the fat kid story and found freedom (and fun) in real food and disco. Since then, he's helped people all over the world lose their fat stories and 3-million-plus pounds.

THE 3 DEMONS: DEPRESSION, ANXIETY, AND ADDICTION

WE ARE WHAT WE THINK, and when we are thinking negative thoughts all day long we become depressed, dreary, anxious, sick, unhappy, dismal, gloomy, wretched, somber, drab, lifeless, insipid little human beings. This soul-destroying way of thinking is where a lot of illness comes from and where the majority of our stress is born.

The thing is, our brains are wired to hold on to negative thoughts for our survival. They remind us where the tiger lives, what plants are poisonous, and what guy screwed us over last year, which can all be helpful. Unfortunately, the brain doesn't work in the same way for positive thoughts. Instead, it picks them up, uses them, and then tosses them by the wayside like a cheap pair of shoes. Poof, they disappear, unless, of course, we consciously pay attention to them. If we notice and take them in, then they'll stay awhile. They might even purchase land right there in the middle of our minds.

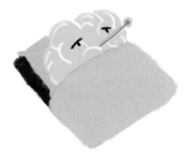

When you are feeling depressed or anxious or are in the throes of an addiction of any kind (booze, shopping, Facebook, Ho Hos, gossip, meth), you should know that these are actually the best times to meditate, although they might also be the hardest. Meditating during the difficult times is how you develop resilience and grit, and if you do it, you will eventually learn that you are way more durable than you thought you were.

The gift of these high-anxiety moments is that if you can bring yourself to meditate during them, you will see that it's a tangible, real-life tool that you can rely on no matter how overwhelming the crisis or how crippling the anxiety. Meditation is real. It stops the free fall. It will change your life.

SWIPE RIGHT

Research has shown that people who tend to be more negative in their thinking have more activity in the left prefrontal cortex of their brains, whereas those who sway toward life's bright side have more activity in their right prefrontal cortex. So if you find yourself sounding like Negative Nancy, all the time, don't worry—meditation will shift that activity from the left side to the right side and turn that frown upside down. Just sit.

STOP FAKING

When someone asks you how you are and you're not doing so well, do you tell the truth or are you one of those "I've never been better" people? If it's the latter, ask yourself, Who am I telling this to? And is it true? It might sound very 1970s kumbaya, but it's time to get in touch with your feelings and out of denial. Part of understanding your story is accepting reality. And part of reality is knowing how and what you are actually feeling. So spend a little time feeling those feelings.

FEEL YOUR FEELINGS: A MEDITATION

This is how you sit your way out of getting hijacked by your thoughts:

1   You sit.

2   You take 3 deep belly breaths.

3   You locate and identify the physical feeling that is operating within you.

4   You feel and experience that feeling in your body.

5   You watch that feeling.

6   You watch what it connects to.

7   You watch the anxiety or depression or pain or all three.

8   You watch the craving.

9   You watch the desire to quash the feeling. Do it again.

10   That's it.

11   Repeat.

GOT NATURE?

What kind of meditation is good for anxiety?

All meditation is helpful. But sometimes anxiety makes you want to run away even from your cushion. Go find a bench, a patch of grass, a tree, a beach, or a mountain to sit near, in, or on and breath. Let nature do its job and use its endless supply of oxygen to anchor your breath and practice. Even something as simple as removing your shoes and touching the ground with your bare feet will recalibrate you. It doesn't matter how cold it is, do it anyway. It's a quick and wonderful way to get outside of yourself.

FAIR-WEATHER FRIEND

When I am in a good space I can meditate no problem, but when things are not so great, it's the last thing I can possibly do.

Meditation when life is good is much easier: there are fewer distractions, there's less stress, the wind is at your back. When life is tough, everything is more challenging, including meditation. But that is exactly when you need it the most.

I've been struggling with depression for years, but I don't want to go on medication. Will meditation help?

Studies say yes, meditation will help big-time. In many cases it helps as much as or more than medication. The catch is, you have to do it.

MEDITATION FOR THE BLUE MONDAYS

ALTERNATE NOSTRIL BREATHING:

1 Sit comfortably and place your right thumb on your right nostril and inhale through the left nostril. Then while holding your breath, close the left nostril with your right pointer finger and release your right thumb and exhale through the right nostril. Inhale through the right nostril while holding your breath and release the left nostril and exhale.

2 Continue, alternating sides.

3 This exercise balances the left and right sides of your brain, reduces stress, and calms the nerves, leaving you feeling clear and alert.

4 Afterward, sit and breathe in and out through both nostrils for a minute or so.

5 Don't think so much about getting it right or think too much about what you are doing. Remember, you are just breathing.

The shit is hitting the fan right now. I was just diagnosed with _____. I'm in a tailspin. I know I need to meditate for health reasons, but I can't get there mentally.

It's incredibly difficult to meditate in the middle of a crisis, especially when you've got that anchorless feeling, which is why we like this simple but powerful grounding meditation. Also, we like it because it works.

MEDITATION FOR WHEN THE RUG GETS PULLED

1   You can either sit down or do this one while standing.

2   Take a long, deep belly breath in.

3   Exhale quickly through your mouth.

4   Take another long, deep belly breath in.

5   Exhale quickly through your mouth (do this until you feel the anxiety lessen, then once it does, start to exhale through your nose).

6   Take another long, deep belly breath in.

7   Now exhale through your nose, extending the exhalation.

8   Continue this for as long as you can. If the anxiety returns, go back to the beginning steps of exhaling quickly through your mouth.

Does drinking delete the positives of meditation?

No, but if you have a drinking problem, you might want to meditate more often (and seek help if needed). And nothing can delete the positives of meditation. The thing about meditation is that you might stop drinking because of it—or at least the self-loathing kind of drinking. But if you want to keep drinking and you want to meditate, so what?

I'm a year sober but still learning how to self-soothe instead of soothing with the sauce. I find myself replacing the booze with hours on Facebook or shopping or eating crap food. How can meditation help with this?

One of the many reasons that meditation is so powerful is that it teaches us to do nothing but sit when horrible uncomfortable feelings arise. This is what it means to self-soothe, to sit with thoughts and feelings that we'd rather quash with booze, TV, Facebook, crap food, or whatever you prefer. Meditation is a practice; you can become more and more comfortable with larger levels of discomfort the more often you show up.

NOTES FROM THE CUSHION

Elizabeth has quit many a thing in her lifetime, including drinking, and meditation played a big role in that journey. It's been a powerful tool in dealing with addiction because it's allowed for her to sit with discomfort instead of attempting to destroy it. Meditation's greatest gift is self-awareness, giving us front-row seats to our own lives.

Do I need a mantra?

A mantra (a word or a phrase) is an anchor for meditation and is especially helpful for people who finds that their breath doesn't hold their attention enough and that their thoughts are running the show. You don't need one, but it's certainly better than the negative chatter we often repeat to ourselves.

NOTES FROM THE CUSHION

What is wonderful about having a mantra is that once you have found yours, you can say it to yourself when you are in the throes of a stressful situation. It will help you to breathe more space into that moment. It's like calling in the destressing brigade. All the breath and calmness associated with that mantra shows up to support you when you really need it.

FINDING OM

How do I find a mantra?

There are lots of popular mantras, but find one that resonates for you, as you will find that it isn't really a one-size-fits-all kind of thing. It doesn't have to be in Pali, the ancient language of the Buddha, or from any sacred text. But it does need to speak to you and come from your heart. It may take trying a few out before one really sticks for you.

MANTRA	MEANING	GOOD FOR
Sat Nam	Truth is my name	Intuition and clarity
Om	The sound of the universe	Feeling oneness
Ram	God	Building your inner fire
Om shanty shanty	Om peace peace	Peace
Om namah shivaya	I bow to God	Letting go
Om mani padme om	I bow to the god inside of me	Wisdom
Hamsa	I am	Ego blasting
Let go	Let go	Letting go
Love light	Love and light	Overcoming obstacles
Lucky duck	To be human is fortunate	Abundance

LOVE EVERYONE

THE CHANTING MAN: KRISHNA DAS

Krishna Das is a Grammy Award–nominated American vocalist who sings kirtan—Hindu devotional amusic. He's got the voice of an angel, and his soulful chants have earned him the title "Yoga's Rock Star." He travels the world with his harmonium, raising vibrations everywhere. He is the master of the mantra and chants his heart out, transforming the world around him to one of love and joy.

We are so programmed to feel that our emotions are the most important thing in the Universe . . . We write, produce and act in the story of me. And then we write reviews—and read them and get more depressed. All we can do is let go, and that comes from training. And then we spend less and less time in the darker spaces.

CHAPTER 7

MEDITATION AND YOU: WHO DO YOU WANT TO BE IN THE WORLD?

DO YOU WANT TO BE HAPPY? UNINTERRUPTED HAPPINESS IS UNCAUSED. TRUE HAPPINESS IS UNCAUSED. YOU CANNOT MAKE ME HAPPY. YOU ARE NOT MY HAPPINESS. YOU SAY TO THE AWAKENED PERSON, "WHY ARE YOU HAPPY?" AND THE AWAKENED PERSON REPLIES, "WHY NOT?"

ANTHONY DE MELLO

MEDITATION AND YOU

Let go of the expectation that meditation has to do something for you. Staying with a practice is a form of faith, it's having a belief that meditation will make your life better. And it will, if you get out of the way and allow it to. Know that meditation is impacting your life even if you can't see it yet.

Many of the reasons that we show up to sit every day aren't revealed to us until much later. We don't always need to know, and getting comfortable with not needing to know is an enormous part of this practice.

NOTES FROM THE CUSHION

We know that we told you that having an intention is incredibly helpful in meditation, and it is, but so is not knowing why you are there in the first place and being open to whatever happens next

Most people sign up for meditation because we want big change, we want to fix things, we want results, and we want to lose a couple of pounds in the process. The truth is, meditation infiltrates every single aspect of our lives. It is the magical, mysterious healer that gives us back our confidence, locates the missing pieces of our self-esteem, and makes it so that we feel comfortable in our own skin. It's been working for people all across the universe for the past 5,000 years.

So ask yourself, who do you want to be in the world? Because meditation will help get you to that part of yourself—if you show up. We promise that if you stay with a practice, you will not only make amends with yourself but you will also find compassion for the whole world.

THE SEED DOES NOT KNOW WHAT THE FLOWER WILL LOOK LIKE

Meditation isn't an escape; real life still happens with all of its craziness, challenges, arguments, traffic jams, spoiled kids, broken hearts, bruised egos, shattered dreams, and red wine spills. Real life can be tough. That stuff won't disappear just because you meditate. But over time you will develop a different level of tolerance for all the shitty days. That's what it means to have faith in the practice, that it will indeed make your life better.

DON'T ADD FUEL TO THE FIRE

It's not meditation's fault if you don't like what is coming up. If horrible feelings about your relationship are coming up, let them. If suddenly you detest your life, so what? Maybe you need a safe place to have these thoughts, so go ahead and give yourself permission to let them out. The trick is to not judge the thoughts or add fuel to them or attach a story to them or make a case against your husband or wife or partner because of them. Just acknowledge them. Then see what happens.

START WITH YOURSELF

Meditation won't repair a broken marriage in 90 days or less. What it will do is shine some light on the real issues. You can't look at your marriage or your life until you've looked at yourself. Once you've looked at and sat with your own baggage, then you will be able to see what you are bringing to the relationship and to the world. That's a beautiful starting point.

But remember, you will not fix someone else by forcing him or her to meditate with you, so don't even go there, especially with your spouse or partner. People change all the time, but only because they change themselves. You will not and cannot change someone else. If there's one way to make the other person resist and shut down, it's to expect or demand change.

Work on you. The magic of meditation is that when you change, so does everyone else around you. If they come to meditation on their own or get inspired because of you, that's great, but don't forget your job is to get you to meditate, and if you do it enough, you won't worry so much about what your spouse or partner does or doesn't do anymore anyway.

HAPPY PEOPLE CREATE HAPPY RELATIONSHIPS . . .

One of meditation's greatest benefits is that it shows us that we need to let go of the desire to control people and events that we have no control over.

Trust us, they will see the difference in you, and everybody wins. Your spouse, partner, significant other, and probably others close to you (even your pooch) will benefit greatly from your meditation practice because it's one of those gifts that loves to give . . . in such ways as: You will probably be a whole lot more patient, present, available, kind, generous, loving, connected, and compassionate, and others will reap these rewards. It can make for better sex, too.

NOTES FROM THE CUSHION

There was a time when Sukey used meditation as an escape as opposed to a tool. She created a perfect hideout from the real world in the midst of crisis. Her advice: Don't do it, it doesn't work. Avoiding pain by meditation isn't much different than using heavy painkillers and booze. It is another form of denial. She also missed out on many of the lessons and opportunities that come with crisis. Instead, feel the feelings and be in your life, no matter how painful or difficult.

WAKE UP!

THE JOLLY JESUIT: ANTHONY DE MELLO

Anthony de Mello, 1931–1987, was an Indian Jesuit priest, psychotherapist, meditator, author, and a world-famous spiritual leader. His books have been a wake-up call for the millions who have read them. He was also a man who wanted everyone else to love life as much as he did.

Imagine a patient who goes to a doctor and tells him what he is suffering from. The doctor says, "Very well, I've understood your symptoms. Do you know what I will do? I will prescribe a medicine for your neighbor!" The patient replies, "Thank you very much, Doctor, that makes me feel much better." Isn't that absurd? But that's what we all do. The person who is asleep always thinks he'll feel better if somebody else changes. You're suffering because you are asleep, but you're thinking, "How wonderful life would be if somebody else would change; how wonderful life would be if my neighbor changed, my wife changed, my boss changed."

We always want someone else to change so that we will feel good. But has it ever struck you that even if your wife changes or your husband changes, what does that do to you? You're just as vulnerable as before; you're just as idiotic as before; you're just as asleep as before. You are the one who needs to change, who needs to take medicine. You keep insisting, "I feel good because the world is right." Wrong! The world is right because I feel good. That's what all the mystics are saying.

TOUGH TIMES: GETTING COMFORTABLE WITH THE UNCOMFORTABLE

All relationships go through calamity. Sometimes it makes sense to stay, sometimes to go, and sometimes to run like the wind, but you can't make a good decision about any of it when you are in the midst of conflict. That's a fact.

Meditation will help you slow down and tread water so that you can resist the urge to demolish everything just so you are no longer in pain. It will quell the need to do something now, because you want out of discomfort.

Unless, of course, there is abuse. If there is, then do whatever it takes to get out of there now. Otherwise, we say sit with it until you are on solid ground. This doesn't mean don't leave ever, but don't miss out on the lessons. Only you know what to do and being extremely still will help you to listen to that whispering inner guide. So sit and pay attention.

This takes patience. Patience upon patience, and then more patience. It's earning your PhD in patience. When you really learn to tread water, then you no longer have to ask yourself when to make a move; the moves will come naturally, and you'll move without question or debate.

BEING LOVE

Start by choosing the relationship and dropping the need to be right. Because the need to be right all the time pushes the other away, causing much more pain. Ouch. It doesn't matter if the other person is mean, passive, argumentative, bipolar, crazy, or just annoying, because being love is not about him or her. It's about you. You being love.

DO CRISIS BETTER

STOP AND ASK YOURSELF:

- [ ] IS THIS SOMETHING I HAVE CONTROL OVER?

- [ ] HOW CAN I SEE THIS DIFFERENTLY?

- [ ] WHAT IS ACTUALLY HAPPENING HERE?

- [ ] IS THIS TRUE?

- [ ] IS THIS SOMETHING I CAN LIVE WITH? DO I WANT TO LIVE WITH IT?

- [ ] IS THIS SOMETHING I CAN SEPARATE MYSELF FROM OR TERMINATE?

- [ ] IS THIS SOMETHING I CAN WORK ON?

- [ ] IS THIS SOMETHING I CAN GET HELP FOR, AND IF SO FROM WHOM?

- [ ] DO I KNOW ANYONE WHO HAS GONE THROUGH THIS OR IS GOING THROUGH SOMETHING SIMILAR?

- [ ] HOW DO I TAP INTO MY INNER KNOWING AND INTUITION FOR GUIDANCE? HINT: MEDITATE.

AND, MOST IMPORTANT, HOW DO I MAKE THIS THE BEST THING THAT EVER HAPPENED TO ME?

HELPFUL HINTS FOR A BETTER RELATIONSHIP

INSTEAD OF   CHOOSE

 BEING HURT   ⟶ GENEROSITY

 WALLOWING IN PAIN ⟶   FORGIVENESS

 GETTING JUSTICE ⟶   MAGNANIMITY

 BLAMING   ⟶   COMPASSION

 COMPLAINING ⟶   TO LET IT GO (FOR REAL)

 EXPECTING LOVE, ATTENTION, TIME ⟶ TO GIVE

 REACTING   ⟶   TO SMILE

HOLDING A GRUDGE   TO REACH OUT AND HUG

 PUNISHING   LAUGHTER

 BUILDING A CASE   TO SEE THE GOOD

 STEWING   LOVE

 SHUTTING DOWN   TO OPEN UP

 NEEDING TO WIN   TO STOP KEEPING SCORE

 PUSHING THE OTHER AWAY TO BRING LOVE IN

 CALLING IT QUITS   TO BEGIN AGAIN

LOVING KINDNESS MEDITATION
PHASE 1
LOVE ME DO

1 Take a comfortable seat.

2 Close your eyes.

3 Take a few deep belly breaths to get you there.

4 Send yourself well wishes. The classic well wishes are:

MAY YOU BE SAFE, MAY YOU BE HAPPY, MAY YOU BE HEALTHY, MAY YOU LIVE WITH EASE

Feel free to choose any of the above or come up with your own.

5 Repeat the well wishes over and over.

6 Just notice what comes up and do not judge it or run with it.

7 Do this for 15 to 20 minutes.

BE NICE TO YOU

I feel weird sending myself well wishes. It feels fake.

In the beginning it might be a little fake. So what? We don't have a lot of skills or practice in being kind to ourselves. Loving Kindness is a good place to start. It will feel awkward for a bit. Keep going anyway.

HATING KINDNESS

I tried this meditation, but all that came up was frustration and anger.

Just watch the frustration and watch the anger. What do they feel like physically? Emotionally? Be kind and patient with this. Many of us feel like we don't deserve such gifts from ourself to ourself. So work on it.

REALITY BITES

I'm not sure how I am supposed to meditate when I am losing my spouse of 20 years and my kids won't speak to me. I need something stronger than Loving Kindness. I feel like I'm losing everything and you're offering me a candy cigarette.

You don't need anything stronger than yourself. Meditate and have faith and start trusting. All the things that we are trying to delete in life—struggle, hardness, difficulty, pain—are the things that make life big and expansive and rewarding, so be in them; otherwise you are going to miss your life. Loving Kindness is exactly what you need.

I hang on to my partners to the point where I almost shape-shift into them. Then they leave. I die. Then I try to start a meditation practice again and heal. Make the cycle stop.

This cycle probably has nothing to do with your partners, except for the fact that they are doing a wonderful job of spotlighting your shit. You need to stop and look at yourself. Meditation will help you to see the pattern, see how you are operating within the relationship, and it will give you the awareness that will allow you to stop and be free.

ALL YOU NEED IS LOVE

THE MIGHTY HEART: SHARON SALZBERG

Sharon Salzberg is a bestselling author, Buddhist meditation teacher, and cofounder of the Insight Meditation Society in Barre, Massachusetts, in 1974. But we like to think of her as the mother of Loving Kindness. She has given many people a very clear path to happiness through the Loving Kindness meditation and offers a modern secular approach to Buddhist teachings, making them accessible to everyone.

LOVING KINDNESS MEDITATION
PHASE 2
LOVE THE ONE YOU'RE WITH

1 Take a comfortable seat.

2 Close your eyes.

3 Take a few deep belly breaths to get you there.

4 Send yourself well wishes. The classic well wishes are:

MAY YOU BE SAFE, MAY YOU BE HAPPY, MAY YOU BE HEALTHY, MAY YOU LIVE WITH EASE

Feel free to choose any of the above or come up with your own.

5 Repeat the well wishes over and over.

6 Just notice what comes up and do not judge it or run with it.

7 THEN, once you feel grounded, think about someone you want to send well wishes to. It could be a mentor, parent, spouse, partner, child, friend, sibling, anyone really. Bring the image of that person into your mind and repeat the meditation above, only with your person in mind instead of yourself. You aren't limited to a person. You can send it to animals, too. Even the planet.

TRUSTY

I was betrayed by my partner and now that the trust has been broken, I can't go back, even though I want to.

You are keeping your partner in the doghouse with your lack of trust. You can either let go and work on things from a place of love (and not from expectations) or stay miserable. Remember, by not trusting you are not forgiving, which hurts you more than anyone. Letting go does not excuse the other's behavior; instead, it frees you up and gives you both a clean space to work in. Meditation will help you to see all the things that are keeping you from letting go.

NOT FOOLING ANYONE

I'm worried that my kids will pick up on how angry I am at my wife. I try to hide it from them, but I still do it unconsciously.

Chances are, everyone is feeling it. You can't contain emotions just toward one person. If you are constantly angry at your partner, you will leak all over the place and be angry at everyone you cross paths with, including your kids. And eventually you will become an angry person.

Instead, take a look at the situation with your wife, acknowledge that you are angry, and decide whether you are going to change it, accept it, or leave the situation. Meditation will be extremely helpful with making that decision.

OUMMiES, OiNGBATS, AND OiMWiTS

We all have difficult people in our lives—some that we are related to, some that we've inherited, some that we're stuck with, and some that we became friends with too long ago to break up with now. The judge-y next-door neighbor, the ultraneedy mom friend, the bromance that you didn't sign up for, the ex that won't go away, the mean best friend, the lying spouse, the jealous sibling, the coworker-saboteur, Debbie downer and her buddy Negative Nelly, and our personal least-favorite: the bully that stayed that way. Actually, they are not as difficult as we like to think; instead they are usually spotlighting our issues, and that never feels good. It's easier to blame someone else.

Once again we are left with a choice: either become a hater or embrace and allow these difficult people to teach us something about ourselves, challenge our perspectives, help us build tolerance for things we don't understand, and experience levels of compassion that we hadn't realized existed.

Who do you want to be?

LOVING KINDNESS MEDITATION
PHASE 3
GOD DON'T MAKE NO JUNK

1 Take a comfortable seat.

2 Close your eyes.

3 Take a few deep belly breaths to get you there.

4 Send yourself well wishes. The classic well wishes are:

MAY YOU BE SAFE, MAY YOU BE HAPPY, MAY YOU BE HEALTHY, MAY YOU LIVE WITH EASE

Feel free to choose any of the above or come up with your own.

5 Repeat the well wishes over and over.

6 Just notice what comes up and do not judge it or run with it.

7 Once you feel grounded, think about someone you want to send well wishes to. It could be a mentor, parent, spouse, partner, child, friend, sibling, anyone really.

8 Bring the image of that person into your mind and repeat the meditation above, only with your person in mind instead of yourself. You aren't limited to a person. You can send it to animals, too. Even the planet.

9 After sending well wishes to yourself and a loved one, bring in person number 3, aka the difficult person. Bring that person into your mind and notice whatever comes up. Watch and send them all blessings and love. May they be well, may they be happy, may they be free from suffering.

NOTES FROM THE CUShiON

If you find this Phase 3 of Loving Kindness too challenging, then before choosing a difficult person, choose a random person. It can be a barista, bus driver, UPS person, someone you saw walking a dog, anyone really. Decide and send the person well wishes. Try that for a few days (or longer if needed), then try the difficult person in the meditation.

STOP THE BURN

I want to find compassion for my horrible ex-friend, but she burned me way too badly. Help.

So what? You don't have to marry her. Send her well wishes and love and good juju, and if you can only do a tiny bit of that, then do that tiny bit.

Most people aren't walking around planning on hurting and destroying other people; they do it through unawareness, and it usually has nothing to do with you and everything to do with them. So with that in mind, let go. It's not easy, but your life will be a million times easier if you let go instead of resenting, hating, and burning.

That energy will suck the life out of you. By letting go, you aren't saying that whatever the other person did is acceptable. You are only saying that you won't let it bring you down.

LOVE THEM MORE

I have a terribly uptight, conservative family. How do I tell them that they are wrong and that their beliefs are dangerous?

Why not just love them more? Choose to see the goodness in them and send them as much love as your little pores will allow to seep through your skin. Sometimes this will be extremely difficult. Sometimes you might have to repeat "love them more" to yourself over and over again. But it is always worth it. There is no need to add more negative energy anywhere, especially at your own kitchen table.

A LIFE OF PURPOSE

THE NOBLE WARRIOR: NELSON MANDELA

South Africa's first black president, Nelson Mandela showed the world what forgiveness and true leadership can look like. If there is anyone who understands what it means to love them more, it was him. After 27 years in prison, he liberated his country and forgave his captors and oppressors.

While Mandela was imprisoned, his wife was sent to jail. She asked for his advice on how to cope.

He replied:

At least, if for nothing else, the cell gives you the opportunity to look daily into your entire conduct, to overcome the bad and develop whatever is good in you. Regular meditation, say about 15 minutes a day before you turn in, can be very fruitful in this regard. You may find it difficult at first to pinpoint the negative features in your life, but the 10th attempt may yield rich rewards. Never forget that a saint is a sinner who keeps on trying.

Pros and Cons

SUPER MARIO'S ADVICE ON RELATIONSHIPS

A LESSON FROM SUKEY'S FATHER, MARIO CACERES

When Sukey and her sister were engaged, Mario asked each of them to write lists of what it was that made them fall in love with their future husbands. He then asked them to make lists of all of the things that were challenging about the grooms-to-be. After the lists were drawn up, he asked his daughters to read them aloud (at different times). He then asked the girls to sign the lists, proving that they each knew what they would be walking into as they strolled down the aisle. Blissfully, they signed and the lists were forgotten. A few years later, Sukey found herself going through some challenging times in her marriage. Her father recommended that she revisit the letter. She did and was shocked to see that that was what she had signed up for.

EXACTLY!

Her husband had not changed. Even though she didn't believe it, there was proof; it was all written down.

CHOOSE MAGIC
YOUR LIFE IS A CONSCIOUS DECISION

Very few people just stumble into a wonderful relationship or a fairy-tale romance (that lasts more than 18 months) or the perfect job or a life in place of their dreams. Some do, but most people who are living the dream are doing it because they made the choice to do it. That's the secret: There is no secret—it's all a choice.

You can be in a relationship with someone and bring all of your baggage and blame with you, then look at them and see yourself, or you can make a very conscious choice that when you look at the other, you are no longer seeing yourself, your shit, and your issues, but instead the love of your life. That's a choice, not something that happens by chance.

BE THE PERSON WHO FEELS LIKE HE WON THE LOTTERY.

WONDERLAND

You don't have to change one thing about your life; you can have a better life right now. Do everything as if it were for the first time. Own it. Own your life, your relationship, your job, your home, your family, all of it.

Your reaction to every single minute of your life is a choice. Meditate on that.

And the more you meditate, the more magic will appear. We promise.

ASK YOURSELF: WHO DO YOU WANT TO BE IN THE WORLD AND WHAT ARE YOU DOING ABOUT IT TODAY?

Barbara, Elizabeth's mother and Sukey's mother-in-law, is the beloved mom of 7 kids and 22 grandchildren. So she does all right on Mother's Day.

This past Mother's Day, she looked out her window and noticed her good friend and neighbor, a widow who lives alone, walking toward her home. Barbara remembered how many women in her neighborhood were in need of some extra flowers that day. She drove to the florist and spent the rest of the day delivering bouquets and sharing stories and laughs with friends.

CHOOSING TO LOVE IS CHOOSING MAGIC.

CHAPTER 8

EXERCISES IN MINDFULNESS: BE IN YOUR LIFE

You might be wondering: What do the 23½ hours a day spent not meditating look like? How do you keep the awareness going when you are away from the cushion, mired in daily life: the stressful job, the scary boss, the screaming kids, the endless bills, the long lines at the grocery store, the dumb fights with your significant other, and all of the other things that shut you down, numb your senses, and dull your heart?

This is where mindfulness comes in.

Jon Kabat-Zinn, the world's go-to guy for mindfulness, defines it as "awareness that arises through paying attention, on purpose, in the present moment, non-judgmentally."

We like to think of it as an elixir, that if you drink enough of it, you'll end up with magical powers, because it heightens everything—all of your senses, your connection with the human race, your appreciation for nature, your focus, your concentration, your creativity, and, most important, your relationship with yourself.

If you want to be in your life, then mindfulness is something that you actually have to do. Walking around the planet aware and awake instead of on autopilot will make you fall in love with the world and your life. The trick is that you have to be present and alive to see it. Like it was for Dorothy when she crash-landed into Oz, all of a sudden your whole world will go from black and white to color, no matter how difficult that particular day may seem.

DAY TRIPPER

Take a mindful walk around the block: walk slowly and deliberately and notice the buildings, nature, homes, people, pets, colors, smells, and sounds that surround you as you stroll. Mindfulness isn't tricky; just observe what's around you. Become a sightseer in your own neighborhood.

NEIGHBORHOOD MINDFULNESS WILL TRANSFORM YOU INTO:

A fledgling ornithologist

An aspiring botanist

A DIY arborist

An amateur architect

A wannabe landscaper

A know-it-all naturalist

A yard-art connoisseur

Maybe even a Peeping Tom
(although we don't condone that)

WHEN YOU SEE THE WORKOUT OWL, PAY ATTENTION! HE REPRESENTS EXERCISES IN MINDFULNESS FOR YOU TO TRY.

ATTENTiON

Mindfulness is a tool that will help you realize that you are the watcher—of everything. Your job is to notice everything around you and not to react. Mindfulness practice is a way to stop the up-and-down feelings that lead to all of our suffering because it slows us down so that we can respond and so we aren't pulled by every hotheaded urge and emotional whimsy.

BFFS: MEDITATiON AND MiNDFULNESS

Meditation will automatically make you more mindful, and mindfulness will enhance your meditation practice. It's not one or the other; they go hand in hand. For the purposes of this book we refer to meditation when on the cushion and mindfulness for everything that takes place elsewhere.

The beauty of mindfulness is that there isn't ever a bad time for it—aside from when you are asleep. Otherwise, it's good stuff all of the time. To get your groove going, try some of the following suggestions for a daily practice.

EARLY-MORNING MINDFULNESS

MAKING COFFEE: Go slowly: open the bag of coffee and take a deep inhale, then proceed as usual.

TAKING THE KIDS TO SCHOOL: Play I Spy with your children on the walk or in the car.

WALKING THE DOG: Try to notice something that you've never seen before in every yard or driveway.

DRIVING TO WORK: Turn off Google Maps and follow a new route.

SHOWERING: Feel the sensation of the water as it hits your body, breathe in the steam, close your eyes, and just feel.

EXERCISING: Observe your muscles working. What hurts? What is achier or easier than normal? Feel your feet on the ground, just feel. Don't zone out to make the time go by; be in it instead.

ALL DAY LONG: Smile at every person you see (unless of course he or she looks like an ax murderer) and see who smiles back.

DON'T FORGET

As aware as we all think we are, most of us tend to forget to be mindful hourly. The more we practice, the more it sticks. The best way to remember to be mindful is to do mindfulness exercises. They are doable, tangible ways to wake up and smell the coffee.

THiS iS iT

Mindfulness is a state of noticing, which is not worrying about the future or lamenting the past. It's a speed bump that wakes you up and puts you in the here and now. It brings you to the present and puts you back in your life.

Mindfulness does not happen all at once; it's a lifelong practice and you will mess up and forget. So breathe and observe. That's all mindfulness is, noticing. It's a gentle energy. Have the intent of doing a better job, of listening, of being present, and then let go and notice everything around you. While you're at it, see what you can do to help others.

Meditation will remind you to be more mindful, and mindfulness will make you a better meditator.

FOR YOUR ViEWiNG PLEASURE

Pick a window to look out of or a spot in your yard that you visit every day at the same time. Spend a real five minutes there. Notice what's changed since the day before. Have the leaves dropped? Flowers bloomed? Birds stopped by? Laundry been hung? Trash been strewn? Cars come and gone? Pigeons had a party? Snow fallen? Make it a part of your day. Change is constant. Let it teach you.

TRY NOT TO SCORE

THE MINDFUL ATHLETE: GEORGE MUMFORD

George Mumford, sports psychologist, meditator, and mindfulness teacher, has worked with Phil Jackson and many teams that have gone on to become NBA champions. He has been called the secret weapon by many NBA superstars, by bringing mindfulness to their games.

His advice:

The best way to score is to try not to score . . . And the best way to be yourself is to forget yourself.

BAD DAY AT THE OFFICE

Every time you feel stressed, angry, rushed, hurt, rejected, or neglected at the office, stop and find one positive thing about the person, the situation, or even your dog. But use each time you feel triggered as an opportunity to breathe and be happy. It's a choice. It might not feel like it at first, so practice.

BUYING TIME

We say that it's possible to expand the hours in the day and not let it all go by so fast. But in order to do so, you must slow down and notice the days and the hours and the minutes and the moments. When you are in the present, time falls away and life becomes 3D and way less flat, and, oh, more fun, too—even when it's shitty.

A RECIPE FOR MINDFULNESS: Do you make dinner? If not, this is a good time to start. Cooking is a perfect opportunity to practice mindfulness. All of the senses can play a role. Let's make a mindful soup, for example.

RECIPE FOR A MINDFUL SOUP:

SIGHT: What are the ingredients? Have you ever really inspected a pepper? A mushroom? A parsnip? Do it now.

SOUND: Listen to the sounds of your soup-making—the peeling of the carrots, the chopping of the onions, the snipping of the parsley sprigs. If you listen closely, there's a whole orchestra playing right there on your countertop.

SMELL: Take a deep breath. What does boiling water smell like? Smell the fresh pasta as you dump it in the pot. Smell the onions, the mushrooms, the pressed garlic, the Calabrian chile, the fresh spinach, and the crushed rosemary.

TASTE: Sample as you cook. Taste the crispy leeks, the snappy peas, the zesty lemons, and the glass of wine that is filling in as your sous chef.

FEEL: Feel the steam on your face, the textures of the vegetables, the heat from the stovetop, the wooden spoon in your hand as you stir, and the love that you are adding to the soup.

THiNK BEFORE YOU SPEAK

Sometimes stupid things just come out of our mouths, not intentionally or with malice—they just pop out. But it doesn't have to be this way. Instead of allowing crazy comments to spew from your lips, especially during heated moments, stop, shut up, and pay attention. Remember, do not judge either.

Then get in the habit of asking yourself some questions, before you open your mouth.

iS iT HELPFUL?

iS iT TRUE?

iS iT KiND?

WHO iS iT FOR?

WHY AM i SAYING iT?

DO i NEED TO SAY iT?

Obviously, you probably won't have time for all of these questions, but one or two can save you a lot of humiliation and heartache.

SiLENT DAY

Pick a day, or half a day, or a couple of hours, when you aren't working or when you don't have many obligations. Don't speak for that amount of time. Listen and be around people, just don't speak. It's also nice to do this with a partner or a friend. Go be in the world, just don't talk. When you don't interrupt, you will notice how much other people shine. Open your ears and find out what you've been missing.

FEELiNG THE HARD KNOCKS

Hard times can either shut you down or open you up. As with everything else, you have a choice in how to respond. To learn from the tough experiences, to grow, to expand, to see the beauty, and to realize that everything is perfect, start by asking yourself these kinds of questions:

WHAT AM i FEELiNG?

WHAT AM i LEARNiNG?

HAVE i BEEN HERE BEFORE?

WHAT'S THE WORST THAT CAN HAPPEN?

WHAT DO i HAVE CONTROL OVER?

WHAT DON'T i HAVE CONTROL OVER?

WHAT'S GREAT ABOUT THiS?

READY, SET, GO

So many of us spend our lives waiting, as if we are still waiting for life to begin. This is it, my friend. You can wait in line or see the magic in the line, make a friend in line, notice something you've never seen before, learn something new, experience something different—all in that very same line.

Even if you are in a waiting room and waiting to be seen, you still don't have to simply wait, nor should you. It is a perfect opportunity to be mindful. What does the room look like, who is in there, what's on the walls? The floors? What's the receptionist's name? What do you know about him? Who else is in the room? Say hello. What kind of music or Muzak is playing? What do the chairs feel like? What's the lighting like? Always be learning.

BACK TO THE FUTURE

Aside from not being at all helpful, living in the future tends to create awful anxiety. Why not look forward to right now, even if right now is as mundane as sweeping the kitchen floor on a Monday afternoon? If you can't look for and find the beauty and magic in this very moment, no matter what it is, you are going to miss about 97 percent of your life waiting for the big things.

If you slow down and see the overflowing stuff happening right here and now, every single thing about your life will change. It's not one switch that sets all of this off, it's a practice. A meditation practice, a mindfulness practice, and an awareness practice. The key word is *practice*. And remembering. And beginning again and again.

Everyday life is filled with magic, no matter how boring you might think it is.

DO YOU HEAR WHAT i HEAR?

Go eat or get a coffee or a drink solo. Observe all of the conversations (yes, eavesdrop) and sounds around you. You'll hear all sorts of good stuff.

WAX ON, WAX OFF

When you have to do something that you dread, especially a chore that you do often, why not think of it as a mindfulness meditation? Instead of resisting and complaining, give in and enjoy.

MOWiNG THE LAWN

RAKiNG LEAVES

FOLDiNG HEAPS
OF LAUNDRY

WASHiNG DiSHES

GARDENiNG

VACUUMiNG

PAiNTiNG A FENCE

JUST THiNK OF THE KARATE
KiD —WAX ON, WAX OFF

CLOSE ENCOUNTERS: HINTS FOR A MINDFUL LIFE

- When you see the first person of the day, notice something you've never seen before.

- When you run into someone you don't like, find something that you adore about that person—whether it's his or her eyelashes, crooked teeth, shoes. There will be something.

- Who in your daily life do you see all the time but still don't know his or her name? Find out what it is.

- In your next conversation with someone, anyone, count to 3 in your head every time he or she is finished speaking before you respond. Notice how much and how often you want to interrupt.

- Acts of kindness: Do something nice for someone you don't know today. Hold a door, give up your seat on the train, buy that person a coffee, or say hello and talk to him or her. Connect.

NOTES FROM THE CUSHION

Bob and Cortney, our brother and sister-in-law, have 7 kids. They make a point to have a family dinner every night if possible, and every night they go around the table and each shares his or her highlight of the day. It keeps everyone on their toes, it keeps them connected, and it makes dinner way more fun.

DEATH TO MINDFULNESS: THE MOBILE PHONE

Truly, there isn't anything much worse to kill your alertness and attention than the evil cell phone.

Coping in the digital age:

THE DINNER GAME: The next time that you are out to dinner with a group of friends, have everyone put their phones in the middle of the table. The first person who picks up the phone pays the bill.

EMAIL TIME: Choose one time a day (two max) that you check and send email. No one will die, and everyone will get used to it if you stand by your rule. It will change your life.

MOBILE ETIQUETTE: Make your own phone rules: put the phone away at meals, at parties, while walking down the street, when with friends, family, or even the pets.

PHONE HOME: One day a month (or more) leave your phone at home and go be in the world. That was the norm not all that long ago. It's called freedom.

USE iT AND LOSE iT: MiNDFULNESS AND WEIGHT LOSS

Mindfulness is not fen-phen, so don't expect any overnight miracles. The reason people drop the pounds when they tune in to their lives is that they catch themselves before they eat that whole gallon of ice cream. Mindfulness is a learned process and it isn't quick, but that's one of the reasons it's so effective.

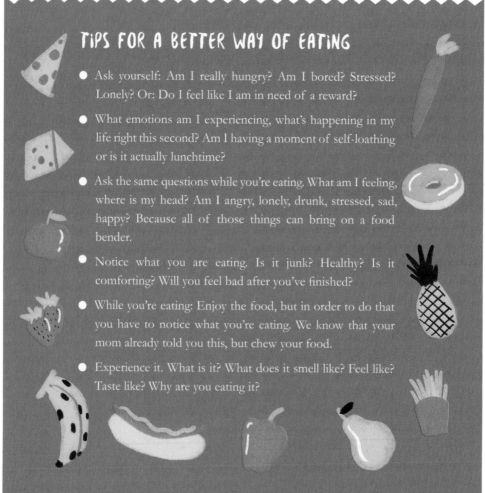

TiPS FOR A BETTER WAY OF EATING

- Ask yourself: Am I really hungry? Am I bored? Stressed? Lonely? Or: Do I feel like I am in need of a reward?

- What emotions am I experiencing, what's happening in my life right this second? Am I having a moment of self-loathing or is it actually lunchtime?

- Ask the same questions while you're eating. What am I feeling, where is my head? Am I angry, lonely, drunk, stressed, sad, happy? Because all of those things can bring on a food bender.

- Notice what you are eating. Is it junk? Healthy? Is it comforting? Will you feel bad after you've finished?

- While you're eating: Enjoy the food, but in order to do that you have to notice what you're eating. We know that your mom already told you this, but chew your food.

- Experience it. What is it? What does it smell like? Feel like? Taste like? Why are you eating it?

NOTES FROM THE CUSHION

French fries aren't so healthy, but like everything else they are fine in moderation. Which is why we celebrate the start of each new month with FRENCH FRY DAY. This takes care of the craving for the rest of the month. Note: This works for any slightly terrible habit.

RUN AWAY

So many of us like to check out when we work out, but it's much more effective and fun (yes, fun) to check in. Feel your feet hitting the ground or your thighs as they pedal away; feel your arms pumping. Also, notice what's around you when you are working out. What sights, smells, sounds are surrounding you. When you zone out, you miss all the good stuff and many of the good effects.

SHOW AND TELL

When you take a walk or go running, take 5 minutes and mentally describe what you are seeing to your faraway friend.

Ellen Langer, a social psychologist, has pioneered mindfulness studies for more than two and a half decades. In a study on mindful exercise, she told 44 hotel chambermaids that their work (vacuuming, cleaning, changing bedding) was the same thing as exercise and that cleaning rooms counted as a daily workout. A month later the group had lost an average of 2 pounds and 10 points off of their systolic blood pressure even though no one was doing anything differently. It was simply doing their work mindfully and seeing the exercise within it that caused the changes.

ONE THING MOST

Multitasking might feel like you are doing more, but you miss a lot. We are wired to focus on one thing at a time, and when we multitask, we get scattered and do less and do it less effectively.

MULTITASKING IS BAD FOR YOUR HEALTH, BRAIN, AND PRODUCTIVITY

IT SLOWS DOWN COGNITIVE SKILLS: The mental going back and forth between tasks reduces attention span, learning, and performance. Because, in fact, we do not multitask, we go back and forth from one task to another and both are accomplished more slowly and in most cases not very well.

IT INCREASES CORTISOL: Increased cortisol makes us tired and stressed. Why? Because the brain doesn't work so well when it is asked to focus on multiple tasks at once.

IT DECREASES IQ BY AS MUCH AS 10 POINTS OR MORE: A University of London study showed that multitasking cognitive tasks lowered IQ as much as if the participants had stayed up all night or smoked pot beforehand.

IT'S ADDICTIVE: When we have a bunch of tiny tasks to finish, we get little hits of dopamine each time we complete one. So it's addictive, even though these tiny goals probably have very little to do with what we are trying to accomplish in the first place.

iT DECREASES EMPATHY: Multitasking diminishes brain density in the part of the brain that is connected with empathy and connection. So it not only makes you distracted, but it also makes you cold and unfeeling. It might feel productive to make phone calls, catch up on email, and help the kids with homework, all while making dinner, but it disconnects us and, ultimately, we miss out.

COUNT YOUR BLESSINGS

THE BiG MAN, AKA POPS: ROBERT NOVOGRATZ

Robert Novogratz, father of 7 kids and grandfather of 22, grew up in a tiny town in Pennsylvania made up of Austrian and Hungarian immigrants. He was an All-American football player for West Point and went on to serve in the army for 30 years. When he was 77, with advanced heart disease, his doctors told him that if he wanted to stick around, he need to change his habits: go vegan, meditate, and no more booze. A big order for a former meat-eating, beer-drinking Austrian football player.

But Robert is a man who is in love with life and with his wife, family, and friends, and so he followed orders, lost 50 pounds, and reversed the heart disease and all of the bad numbers that went with it.

When asked the secret for all of his happiness, he says he counts his blessings every day.

THE DOLDRUMS

Using mindfulness to beat the blues. Hints for the difficult days:

- Remember, life is here to teach you. It's all lessons. Every sadness, anxiety, or annoyance is spotlighting something in you. Take the time to investigate it, note it. You can even say bless this anger or bless this sadness. Detach from it and observe.

- Stop letting mundane nonsense get you down. It only takes a tiny bit of awareness to get on the other side of that kind of stuff. If you miss the flight, get in a fender bender, or are late for work, remember that it's all a choice in how you see it and respond.

- See everyone with goodness. In every challenging situation, make it your job to find what is good in the person or people or situation. If you look for the good or the lesson, you will see it.

TIPS FOR BEING IN YOUR LIFE

- Talk to strangers (and smile, too).
- Go for a hike, or a walk, or a stroll, but get some nature.
- Make cookies for the new people on your block (even if they moved in 10 years ago).
- Go to a silent disco or, even better, host one.
- Invite people for dinner.
- Write a love letter.
- Pet a dog.
- Think benevolently and if you have any sort of generous thought, no matter how crazy or big, do it.
- Give an honest compliment.
- Call your mother.

SUPERSEER

We have a friend named Anna who is constantly running into people she knows, people from her present and from her past. She can be anywhere in the world and voilà, she sees her freshman-year roommate's parents on a subway or her best friend's hairdresser from Seattle at a coffee shop. So, after hearing about scores of these incidents, we Googled the phenomenon. And we found out that it's a thing. Anna, along with 2 percent of the population, is a super-recognizer, a person with an uncanny ability to recognize faces, even faces they've only seen once or only seen years before.

Hours after figuring this out, we were walking down a busy New York City street when she yelled "Mark" to a guy across the street. He looked confused until she responded, "Hey, it's Anna. We met on the flight to Miami last Christmas." He smiled and said hello. Just another super-recognizing moment for her.

The moral of this story? We all run into people as often as Anna does, it's just that the majority of us miss them; we don't recognize the people we know or knew. So what else are we missing?

JUST SIT

We hope that you either have started to meditate or will start as soon as you close this book. We weren't kidding; it changed our lives and we promise it will change yours, too, but only if you actually sit. Remember, you can do it anywhere, anytime, without a whole lot of hoopla. Just sit.

UNDER A WILLOW TREE

AT THE PYRAMIDS

AT A PROTEST

AT AN ART MUSEUM

IN A CAVE

WITH YOUR CAT IN YOUR LAP

WHILE FEEDING THE BABY

ON AN AIRPLANE

IN A PASTURE

ON A ROOFTOP   IN THE BACK OF A TRUCK   IN A CANOE

IN THE GARDEN   AT THE LIBRARY   AT THE NAIL SALON

AT A LAUNDROMAT   AT THE AQUARIUM   ON THE BEACH

YOUR
IMAGE
HERE

YOUR
IMAGE
HERE

YOUR
IMAGE
HERE

ABOUT THE AUTHORS

SUKEY AND ELIZABETH NOVOGRATZ are two of the founders of the celebrated newsletter *The Well Daily*. Together they have traveled the world to study meditation and learn from its many renowned teachers. Elizabeth is the coauthor of *Downtown Chic* and *Home by Novogratz*, and lives in Brooklyn, New York. Sukey is an executive producer of the acclaimed documentaries *The Hunting Ground* and *I Am Evidence*. She sits on the board of the Joyful Heart Foundation and lives in New York City.

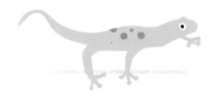